2009 SELL YOURSELF ON PAPER WITH A COMPETITIVE RÉSUMÉ-COVERLETTER COMBINATION

By David Francis Curran

This book is dedicated to Patricia. Who made sure the interviewing area was always ready for clients. And to all those clients who taught me so much about writing to sell.

© David Francis Curran

Introduction

The résumé and cover letter today are an integral part of finding a job. They are the tools that hint to a prospective employer that you might be of value to him. They are the lures that catch the employer's interest and get you that all-important interview, so careful writing is important.

Yet as important as the résumé and cover letter are, the writing of a résumé and cover letter is unfortunately not an exact science. It might be better to think of it as a form of advertising in which the product you want to sell is yourself.

You start out with a disadvantage. You simply don't continually sell yourself to the job market. You were either employed, or in school or being a housewife or something else. So your résumé and cover letter combination are always a "new" advertisement rather than a "time tested" one. As such your résumé is always more of a marketing experiment than a "sure thing." There are far too many people in the world both employer and employee to predict what response a given application will receive in any given situation. For this reason (though many so called résumé experts fail to be able to fathom this) it is inane to insist that one particular form of presentation is absolutely correct and another absolutely wrong.

In this guide to putting together a selling résumé-cover letter combination rules and generalizations are stated based on what I've found in my professional résumé writing experience to be the most valuable ideas on competitive résumé writing. These ideas are based on, professional experience (most of my clients reported better than 50% interviews), analysis of available data (I borrowed any good idea I could find), extrapolation of the laws of parallel arts, (I'll be explaining what I've learned about selling), and experiment (I was my own guinea pig as were my first customers but I survived and so did they.) I've tried to give explanations wherever possible so that you can decide which choices will be of greater value to you given your circumstance. Your individual input must be the final word in creating a successful résumé and cover letter of your own.

HOW LONG WILL IT TAKE TO WRITE UP YOUR RÉSUMÉ AND COVER LETTER?

Usually, one of the first questions clients asked me when calling to inquire about a professionally prepared résumé was how long would it take. This was usually followed by a comment that went "...because I saw this ad in today's paper." Although I could prepare a résumé overnight, you, if you are planning on preparing your own should give yourself a few days for the project. I'll comment about rushing to apply to ads in "today's" paper a little later on.

Even when I was fully into professional résumé writing I did my best work when I allowed time for revision. When you putting together your own résumé it good to keep in mind that for all practical purposes the résumé is the first representation of you an employer sees. And in case you weren't aware of it, communication scholars have found that most people in this country tend to favor their negative impressions of people over their positive ones and tend to stick with the first impression they have. A sloppily done résumé, (and here I also refer to sloppiness of content as well as appearance) can ruin your chances with an employer from the start. The idea behind the résumé is to sell yourself and to do that you must start with a good impression.

Thus for the beginning résumé writer I recommend "Enough time - but not too much." A limit of five days would be appropriate. Too little time will result in a hastily written résumé. Too much time tends to have the writer looking aimlessly for something better than his or her best.

A GOOD FIVE-DAY SCHEDULE WOULD BE:
- One day for reading and collecting facts about yourself.

- One day for revising those facts and selecting which will go into your résumé.
- One day for the initial writing.
- One day for revision.
- And one day for the final draft and proofreading.

Typing and printing time is not included in the above schedule. The schedule itself including typing and printing will be discussed later on in greater detail.

BUT WHAT ABOUT THE AD IN THE NEWSPAPER YESTERDAY?

Getting a good competitive résumé and cover letter combination to the employer is far more important than getting a résumé there within a day or two of the first appearance of a job ad in the newspaper. There are a number of reasons for this.

First, you may be proving your over-anxiousness by arranging to be first to have your résumé on the employer's desk.

Second, the mails are at times fickle and Express Mail is an expensive way to apply for jobs.

And third, though the first sometimes stand out, having your résumé arrive in the middle of the search has little advantage, specially when résumés that come before and after yours seem just as good. Because most people try and get their résumés in fast after the appearance of a job ad, the result is a landslide of résumés for the typical "good" job ad within the first few days of its appearance. Repetition of an ad in consecutive Sunday papers may increase the response. The result may be a period in which overworked assistant personnel managers may not be able to discern it from the hordes of others. Résumés, unsurprisingly, have been known to get lost during this time. So, the worst part of all about being first or in the middle of the application rush is that you may be forgotten in the ensuing avalanche of applicants.

The more important a job's responsibilities are the less likely the employer is to fill it with the first available body. There are exceptions but this is a good general rule. And it means that employers tend to do some looking before making a decision. Chances are they will still be deciding after the ad for the job is no longer running in the newspaper (or whatever medium they chose to advertise it.)[i] It may just pay to come in on the end of the line. Especially since there are many people who give the most attention to the last arguments they hear.

As far as exceptions go there is only one. The company may find the search too costly, or time consuming and pick a candidate early. Otherwise, if a company is in a big hurry it will probably use an employment agency. Keep in mind that if a company feels a position is easy to fill they might not think highly of the person they hire to fill it.

So call the company. Tell them you'd like to apply and ask them if they will tell you their employee search deadline so that you can be sure to get your résumé in on time. Then apply near the end.

PART ONE: THE RÉSUMÉ

The résumé and cover letter are most effectively used in combination to generate interest. However, each should ideally generate interest in the applicant on their own. Because of this I will discuss the résumé first so you be able to appreciate the elements that make for its effectiveness. Once you know how to create an effective résumé I'll show you how to enhance its selling power with the cover letter.

THE FUNDAMENTAL RULES OF RÉSUMÉ WRITING

My fundamental rules of résumé writing are a combination of things I learned from creative writing and advertising. How to apply them will be explained within the body of the text. But I think it is a good idea that you have a basic understanding of them now. That way, you can use them to judge the value of your own ideas as you read on.

THE FUNDAMENTAL RULES
1) The main task of your résumé is to ATTRACT ATTENTION. In some cases your résumé may be one of hundreds on an employer's desk. You must grab the employer's attention in the first few seconds. If you don't you may never get another

chance.
2) While attracting attention you should at the same time GENERATE INTEREST so that your reader is induced into reading further.
3) Your résumé should CREATE AN OVERALL IMPRESSION. The impression you are striving for is "I am the one for the job." The most successful theme to use in your résumé to convey that impression is covered in the next section.

THE MOST SUCCESSFUL THEME YOUR RÉSUMÉ CAN HAVE

The most important aspect of your résumé, the thing that can attract attention and generate interest, is the attitude about yourself the résumé conveys. Yet a healthy attitude is not enough. You must have the proper job-finding attitude.

In order to illustrate what this attitude is, I used to tell my clients the following true story.

I had just dropped out of a graduate school program[ii] and was looking for a job. My father sent me to see an ex-student of his. The man was the sales manager of one of the largest textile manufacturing firms in the country and he gave me the most valuable advice I ever received about job hunting.

"There was a fellow here in the office the other day," the sales manger told me, "and I asked him why he wanted to be a salesman?"

"He said, ""Well I like to travel and meet people and I get along with people real well so I can talk to them. I think it would be a job I could really enjoy.""

"Do you know what I felt like telling that guy?" the sales manager asked me.

"I don't know," I said. "He sounded like he'd be a good salesman to me."

"Well, I felt like telling him to get the hell out of my office." the sales manager said.

"Why?" was all I could say because I was very surprised.

The only reason," the sales manager said, "That I want to hear from someone coming in and asking for a job in sales is: that they can make money at it, and therefore I can make money by hiring them."

If you have not already recognized it as such, you had better now realize you live in a competitive world. And to get ahead in it you had better be willing to compete.

Far to many people have this attitude: "Well I'm a nice person and I think I might like that job and won't you please give it to me?" or "I have experience at this kind of job and could you look at my background and figure out that I would be a good employee for you." They write résumés that show this is their attitude and for some reason, call it shyness or stupidity or whatever this is all they ever do. But what chance do these "nice people" have against other people who say: "I want that job because I can do it so well we can both profit."

No matter what the job, whether it be sales manager or hospital attendant, the job contest is between those applicants who show they believe they will be successful in such a way that their profit means the company will profit also.

Employers will never be impressed with YOUR NEEDS. They will not be impressed if you make them WORK HARD TO SEE IF YOU MIGHT FIT IN. It cannot matter to a practical businessman that you would "enjoy" the work or that you are a "nice" person who needs a job.

The proper job finding attitude is that you know you have something to offer, that you know you can apply yourself to the job you are seeking in such a way that both you and your employer will profit. And that you are aware this is your selling point.

Presenting your qualification in light of this attitude is the most successful theme your résumé can have.

The rest of this book is geared toward developing this theme in your résumé and cover letter.

PARTS OF THE RÉSUMÉ

The Identification and Heading

The first thing to do in creating a résumé is to present the prospective employer with information as to who you are.

Your résumé, in which printed characters communicate a message, is a form of graphic art. The graphic design (in this case the arrangement of characters on a page) of your résumé can help attract attention, generate interest and create a good impression about you.

In the many books written on job-hunting a great many graphic variations on the simple process of identifying one's self have been expounded upon. Here I will present just a few variations.

I do this for the sake of simplicity. graphic design possibilities are endless and at times hard to choose from. They can be hard to choose from because, by themselves, one good design can have little advantage over another. The only real advantage might be a form an employer likes that he has not seen before or one that he does not see often. But there is no way you can tell what that form would be.

The arrangements in all the sections of this book were chosen because they work well together graphically. The typeface for this book is 'courier 'and it was chosen because it is the standard typewriter font where each character takes up the same amount of space. (i.e. an 'I' takes up the same space as an 'M.') This was necessary here to ensure some consistency in design for our examples. However, you may use any font and you may find some benefit to working with your own design. Keep in mind newer typefaces take up space according to their shape (i.e. an 'i' takes up less space then an 'm'.) With the newer typefaces you can get more on a page. However with a face like courier, it can be easier to position text on a page. The thing to remember is that if you change typefaces you may have to reformat your résumé as the position of the words on the page may change drastically.

As a professional, I found my time best spent concentrating on content within the bounds of a familiar format. And you might do well to follow suite.

NOTE: In headings full sentences are not required and in fact take up more room than is useful. The convention is to use sentence fragments as long as they make sense.

IDENTIFICATION

Simple:

John C. Francis
12 East Cushman Ave.
Nothview, WI 54952   Telephone (414) 555-1038

With a business phone:

John C. Francis   Telephone:
12 East Cushman Ave.   Business (414) 555-1043
Northview, WI 54952   Home   (414) 555-1038

Permanent address included:

John C. Francis   Permanent Address:
12 East Cushman Avenue   192 Chippewa Road
Northview, WI 54952   Yonkers, NY 10910
414) 555-1038   (914) 555-9991

With a complete business Address:

John C. Francis
12 East Cushman Ave.
Northview, WI 54952   Telephone (414) 555-1038

Business Address:
Ace Cement Company   EMAIL XXXXX@YYY.com
191 East Proust Street   (414) 555-1043 ext. 249
Northview, WI 54952

With pronunciation for difficult names:

Peter Ksneau
(Peter Cans-ow)
134 Pier St.
Yonkers, NY 10910   Telephone (914) 555-9086

   A pronunciation can be very helpful as some people at too proud to admit they would not be able to pronounce your name. A good résumé makes everything as easy as possible for the would-be employer.

THE HEADING

The heading is a small advertisement, a selling introduction at the top of your résumé designed to create interest in you. It can be broken down into two parts, the objective and the body.

YOUR OBJECTIVE

I like to assume in résumé writing that there are two different states of being as far as you and the prospective employer are concerned. The first is what you are, and the second is what you want to be.

If you are seeking the same type of position that you currently hold and are experienced, your résumé's heading might look like this.

"HEAD HUNTER"
Skilled communicator with 6^{iii} years intense local experience in making successful job placements for the Wisconsin Job Service, desiring to combine experience and knowledge in a highly profitable career in management consulting.

In this case the position for management consultant (i.e. an employment agency salesperson who specializes in bringing employee to employer for a fee paid by one or both) was described in a newspaper ad as being for a "Head Hunter." Because the phrase was used in the paper it was used in this heading. Yet, because he had experience in the field he did not describe the position as an objective. Compare the above to the example below in which the applicant has no real experience in the field but would like to get into a new type of work.

Objective: BOY'S CLUB BASEBALL COACH

>Dedicated high school and college baseball star with professional goals in boy's athletics, presently finishing his B.S. in physical education on a part time basis after an honorable discharge from military service.

In the above the applicant was not a coach but desired a position in coaching.

The word "objective" can be valuable in many other ways. It can imply that you will not take a position without advancement opportunities, or that you wish to use your skills in a different job than the one you have been doing. Its beauty (of which you will see more in the sample résumés to come later) is that it can say so much, so simply.

Whether you use the word "objective" or simply describe your professional "being," your heading is the lead phrase in your own personal advertisement. It is who and what you are, and what you want to be.

THE BODY OF YOUR HEADING

Though you may find the heading fairly easy because you know what you want to be or do, the body may seem a bit more difficult. Here you must write a personal advertisement that will convince an employer not only to read further but also to eventually grant an interview.

This fact is brought out in an ad by one résumé writing firm that begins "10 seconds may be all the time you have to attract an employer's attention." The more résumés that cross an employer's or personnel director's desk the less time that person will have to look carefully at each one. After awhile the résumés may begin to look alike, and being human that employer or personnel director is not going to feel like taking a great deal of time to see if you are offering what they want. If they don't see what they want in the first few seconds, your résumé will be dismissed without a second thought.

So the body of your heading must be an attention grabber. It must entice the reader to read on. The best way to do this is to present your best points in a straightforward easy-to-read manner that implies you are the one to meet that employer's needs.

SOME GOOD WAYS TO IMPLY YOU ARE THE ONE

First start off with action words like:

aggressive
innovative
productive
dynamic
profit-oriented
creative
team-worker
self-starting
skilled
hard-driving
etc.

Virtually all the "work" in the world is action-orientated in some way so even a sleeper in a window mattress display had better be "sound-sleeping."

What you want to do is mention those action qualities of yours that will apply to the job you are seeking. For example, a salesman might be "aggressive", if he works alone he must be a "self-starter", and if he had a history of successful sales he must be "highly skilled in sales closings."

Let's just see how that might look on paper.

SALESMAN
Aggressive, self-starting salesman, skilled in closings...

This beginning for the salesman's résumé gives any prospective employer the idea of action. Have you ever heard of an employer trying to hire a dead salesman?

But action words are not the only thing the body of your heading could or should have. A summary of the total experience you will be bringing to your new job can be just as valuable in impressing an employer.

Objective: PERSONNEL MANAGER

    Military officer with over 23 years of diverse experience...

If, however, you have had little experience that could be of use to you in your new job, the heading is not the place to mention a lack of it.[iv]

Other things can be used to enhance your salability in the heading of your résumé. For example, you may want to emphasize your education. In order to judge whether your education is important you should consider it the part it plays in your goals. If you have a Ph.D., and M.S., or even a
B.S. in chemistry and the position you want calls for a degree you'd better mention it in the heading. However, if your education was a B.A. in liberal arts and you have had 20 years of factory supervisory experience the degree is far outweighed by the experience and mentioning it could add nothing to the heading. One rule of thumb would be the more recent the graduation the more valuable the degree. This goes for the high school graduate as well as for the Ph.D. But as you gain experience in any field your education begins to take second place to the experience. Only special education and/or specialized degrees need be mentioned if your experience is significant.

               Private Investigator
Experienced investigator with 10 years experience in all phases of corporate and domestic investigations with an MS in Forensic Psychology….

However, if you don't have at least a college

degree, try to avoid mentioning education, unless that recent education is the only significant experience you have.

Some Examples:

1) A High School Dropout

PRODUCTION SUPERVISOR

Expert troubleshooter with 12 years of production experience as a line supervisor...

2) A Young High School Graduate

Objective: SECRETARY

Responsible high school graduate/honor student, typing 55 WPM, able to take dictation and ....

3) A College Graduate

ADVERTISING SALES

Profit-oriented self-starter with a very successful record as Ad Manager of the University of Oregon's Weekly Ledger, desiring to combine sales, supervisory, problem solving and decision making ability with a journalism degree to effect a highly profitable career.

4) An Advanced Degree

SENIOR COSMETIC CHEMIST
M.S. with 6 years experience in cosmetic formulation...

In your heading body you might like to point out the areas in which your expertise and talent lie if it is not likely to be obvious from the heading alone. For example:

CHIEF EXECUTIVE OFFICER
OR VICE PRESIDENT

> Corporate Vice President of the Thermoplastic Sales Division of the Bubo Corporation, responsible for increasing sales in the past 5 years over 400%, desiring to use his expertise and management ability to insure the profitability of the sales division of a plastics corporation.

If you're in sales you might want to give an idea of the dollar volume you are capable of generating. There are a number of ways to do this.

For example you could mention a percentage figure based on your average yearly increase.

> ... Averaging a 20% increase in sales volume each quarter...

Or you could give a more recent increase if it was your largest.

> ... Increased sales revenues by 80% in the last year....

Some sales people, of course, do well without really increasing their yearly volume by any appreciable amount. Some hard working salesmen have sold so well to their territories there is no one else to sell to, or have so many clients that they have no time for new customers. In this case a yearly or monthly sales figure might be appropriate.

SALESMAN

> Aggressive, self-starting salesman skilled in closings with average yearly sales at $950,000...

Another method is to use statements such as,

"doubled the size of the company in just five years." Long-term achievements should also be described along with shorter term success.

Obviously, the types of things you should mention in your résumé's heading are the things about you that make you look good. You should be honest but is expected that you'll be serving your best stuff on your best plates. So don't fail to mention those cost savings, new methods or whatever you've accomplished, or contributed to.

Now you might consider that few people in their everyday conversation would refer to themselves as aggressive or self-starting. You might think it, but you would not ordinarily say it in ordinary conversation. You might consider it the type of description our greatest admirer might make. Yet in your résumé where you are talking about your talents you have to be your own favorite fan. In your résumé YOU ARE SUPPOSED TO TOOT YOUR OWN HORN.

Employers will expect a fairly honest evaluation of our strong points within a humanly egotistical build up. (That is they will expect it from a good résumé writer.) If you are timid instead of aggressive try "hard-working" to describe yourself. Just keep in mind that the heading is the place to say quickly how good you are. If you can do that well the rest of your résumé will be easy.

SHOWING GOALS

In some cases it will be enough to show in your résumé heading those points about yourself which you feel will draw attention to ourselves.

RESEARCH AND DEVELOPMENT CHEMIST
Innovative team worker responsible for patents involving over $2 million in polymer processing. M.S. degree, Oregon State with intentions toward a doctorate.

While in another case you might want to show where your goals lie if you desire a position you have not already held.

Objective: TRUCK DRIVER

    Recent graduate of Ace Semi-School ranking 10th in a class of 53, with 400 on road hours and a clean driving record, desiring a profitable career in commodity transport.

Describing our goals at the end of the heading can be a good way to describe those goals we consider long term. This is especially true when we feel that using such a goal as an immediate objective might seem a bit forward.

                SALESMAN
Hard-driving self-starter, a recent graduate whose successful part time sales earnings financed his B.B.A., desiring a rewarding career in a growing company with long-term management opportunities.

In the above example the salesman's true objective was management. However he felt that he would have a better opportunity if he started in a company as a salesman.

A SKELETON HEADING

Your objective and heading body should look like the skeletons below. (Allowing, of course, for your own rearrangement, subtractions and additions.)

                WHAT YOU ARE
Qualities --- What you are, experience and/or Education and/or accomplishments. (Plus long term goals if different from objective.)

Objective: WHAT YOU WANT TO BE

Qualities --- What you are presently, what Experience and/or education and/or accomplishments you expect to use in obtaining goal. (Plus a more exact description of your goal is you feel it is needed.)

Further examples will be found in the résumé example section.

NEWSPAPER ADS

Before we go on to the body of the résumé itself it might be a good idea to cover how the objective and heading can be arranged to fit advertisements (job ads) in a newspaper, online, or wherever you may find them.

Compare the following:

Objective: EDITOR

               Experienced self-publisher with national writing credits, expert in all phases of publishing: Editing, photography, graphics, and press law, currently earning a B.S. in Journalism in a self-paced program.

Imagine that after sending out a résumé with the above heading the following ad appears in the job section of the local Sunday paper.

WANTED COMMUNICATION SPECIALIST. The Bubo company is looking for a communication specialist to handle the ad promotion of its chemical product line. The ideal candidate will have knowledge of Graphic Arts & Photography and be a skilled communicator. interested applicants should send their résumés to...

This is how our editor's heading might be changed to fit the ad in the paper.

               COMMUNICATION SPECIALIST

EXPERTISE: Written Communication & Oral Presentations

Skills: Paste Up, Layout, Design, Photography,

Black & White Darkroom, Blueprint Reading, Typing, Microcomputer Operation, Budget Control & Cost Estimating.

This skilled communicator currently with a B.S. in chemistry and earning a degree in news-editorial journalism in a self-paced program has the comprehensive ability to understand the technical aspects of production and the diverse communication skills to weave those aspects into a workable selling program.

You noticed that my previous suggestions for the body of the résumé were abandoned to fit the needs mentioned in the newspaper ad. This is not to suggest that the original was not a good strong heading. My only purpose was to show how with a little creative imagination you could present the information of interest to the writer of that particular job ad in the heading.

The idea of fitting your heading to a job ad is one which requires no special rules. It is merely a matter of selection. You select the attributes the ad asks for or state your talents in a way that implies they can be applied to the job in question profitably. For example, the ad above for a communication specialist did not call for any degree, however, the applicant used both his chemistry degree and his forthcoming journalism degree profitably.

In some cases the job ad that attracts your attention might ask for a skill or experience that you did not emphasize in your original heading.

Consider this original:

> SECRETARY
> Experienced office organizer with over 14 years of diverse, responsible office handling, skilled in dictation, shorthand and typing (55 WPM.)

The ad said:

WANTED GAL FRIDAY: Local executive is seeking an experienced Gal Friday. This could be a rewarding experience for a person with excellent typing and steno skills in addition to a highly developed talent for meeting clients. Contact...

So this was the revised résumé heading:

GAL FRIDAY

Responsible office organizer with over 14 years experience in office handling and direct customer contact public relations, skilled in shorthand and typing (55 WPM.)

In the second example above our secretary has emphasized the skills the employer has asked for in his ad. This is not to imply that the applicant has made up the skills. It might be that this applicant's experience in direct contact public relations was no more than the normal secretary's meetings with her bosses or clients. But often the only difference is the attitude by which your judge your skills, and you have every right to emphasize any point in your experience as gloriously as you can.

Remember the idea of your résumé is to help get an interview. It may be difficult in a short newspaper ad for an employer to paint an exact picture of what he wants. In the interview the secretary above can layout the limits of her experience and ability. However, she would be foolish to assume that her average 14 years of experience would not qualify her. The employer's ad could mean that he wants someone with just her background.

One benefit of doing your heading after reading a "Help Wanted" ad is that the ad can often give you ideas about skills you might not have thought to list in the first place. But never limit the contents of your résumé by what you read in "help wanted" ads or use them exclusively. Ads are not the only sources of jobs and some authorities feel that they represent only a minor percentage of those jobs actually filled.[v]

THE LENGTH OF YOUR HEADING

A good general rule for your heading is that it should not be so long that it takes more than a few seconds to read.

For good measure I've thrown in a few other simple rules that can be broken if need be.

1) Unless trying to fill an otherwise sparse page make the body of your heading at least 40 characters wide (40 spaces on a typewriter or word processor.)

2) Try and have no less than 3 lines or no more than 8.

3) If you have more than 8 lines, break up the lines with an extra space between paragraphs (see the COMMUNICATION SPECIALIST heading previously discussed) - space considerations will be discussed later.

THE BODY OF YOUR RÉSUMÉ

One of the first things to consider as far as the body of your résumé is concerned is whether your résumé is being submitted in confidence. That means you don't want the prospective employer to contact your present employer.

If you do not wish the company you are applying to, to contact the company you work for you, put in the body of the résumé a statement to that effect.

      (Résumé Submitted in Confidence)
or

(Employer not to be contacted at this time)

You should keep in mind that this is only a request and carries little legal clout.

In answering any ad or sending out any résumé you should be aware that you are taking a risk. For example, once after just accepting a advertising sales job for a large Wisconsin newspaper, I was tempted to apply to an even larger newspaper whose "help wanted" ad appeared at the time the first paper hired me. I actually prepared a résumé but forgot to mail it. It was well I did. I learned soon after starting for the smaller paper that both papers were owned by the same company.

Blind box advertisements can present various challenges and these will be discussed in depth a little later on. For now, just be assured if you are dealing with a reputable firm and reputable people your request to keep your application confidential will most likely be honored. Any legitimate business firm, if they acquired a reputation for tattling on people who wished to change jobs would soon find themselves out of the competition as far as the better, but employed, applicants go. All you need do is make sure that the prospective employer knows of your wishes. For this reason I suggest your request to keep your résumé confidential go in the body of your résumé as near to the name and address of your present employer as possible.

SOME RULES TO HELP CREATE A RÉSUMÉ BODY THAT GIVES A GOOD IMPRESSION

Your résumé should be easy to read. Not only in the sense of vocabulary and sentence structure (see Clarity) but in the sense of the spacing of its sentences and paragraphs. If possible the pages should not be gray - an expression in journalism which means that a page has so many black characters on it that at a distance it gives the illusion of being a gray painted page-- which signifies to many people tedious reading. The one way to avoid this is to leave areas of white space on your page.

The length itself will be determined by:

- The number of interlocking concerns. That is the

number of explanations or descriptions which must be made to make clear all of the résumé entries. For example, the statement, "...was responsible for updating procedure based on knowledge acquired as a Military Policeman." in your résumé would require a description of the chief's military experience if it is to be understandable.

- When considering what is important enough to include: remember the résumé is not the place to tell your life story. But it is the place to give a thorough overview of your experience and talents. If you feel something would be of interest to an employer include only enough of it to whet his appetite.

- The number of pages in your résumé will influence the impression it creates. The more complex the "responsibilities" the longer the résumé needed. A truck driver might never need more than a one page résumé. Yet a candidate for the company presidency might not be able to get by with less than four.[vi]

Here are some Guidelines:

a) The one page (sometimes "cram-packed" résumé) offers the most advantages. Because it is familiar it draws the appropriate attention to itself. There are no other sheets to be lost. It may not seem as imposing to the tired résumé-reading employer. Printing and mailing costs are kept down. And finally the limited space will prompt you to use it wisely.

b) Two pages can be used when there simply is too much for one page. But if two pages are used it is best to try and balance information between the two pages. (Printing both sides of a single sheet can be a good idea.)

c) If you have 3 pages you might as well go onto 4. (Although two sides of 8-1/2" by 14" legal paper might work for some three 8-1/2" by 11" page résumés.) Any advantage you have in the shorter résumé is lost after two pages so you may as well put in as much info as you can. When dealing with 3 pages or more, the 11" by 17" sheet really starts to become practical. Many résumé books I read when I was first learning the business suggested that if you did use but 3 pages of an 11 x 17 sheet (which when folded would then yield 4 pages) the remaining blank page could be used for the cover letter. But I personally believe if the cover letter is printed on a printed résumé it might lose the very important personal touch that will be discussed later.

d) The four page résumé should not be used unless you are sure that what you have to say will be so interesting to an employer he'll be willing to read four pages. In some positions, such as vice-presidencies, people may feel four pages would be required. But the material must be "worth reading" even for those exalted positions.

In the four-page résumé special care is required with each page. That is it should be arranged so that when the employer reaches the end of the each page he is encouraged to go on.

If you use 11" x 17" paper folded into a 4-page booklet, care must be taken that the lines on each page line up with those on opposite pages. If you own a word processor and are using your own printer to print individual copies you might be better off printing them on individual sheets of paper and using a folder.

And although a single page résumé can be put on any bond paper, with a 4 page résumé a thicker paper is needed to prevent the print on one side from showing through. A 60 pound bond (at least) is suggested.

CLARITY

Your résumé must be clear and concise presentation of those things that will attract the employer's attention to you and convince him that your talents are valuable.

The heading was the place where the employer's

attention was attracted. The body of the résumé is the place where you are going to back up what you said. To do this adequately the first thing to remember is that clear and simple expression can go a lot father than 20-dollar words. If your résumé reads like Einstein's theory of relativity to the unscientifically educated, the befuddled personnel manager may simply lose interest in you. Your résumé should be produced for a general audience. This does not mean that it should not contain any of the esoteric terminology particular to your line of work. What it means is that the basic structure of your résumé should contain information understandable to all. After laying out a good basic structure the necessarily esoteric aspects of your experience can be added in such a way as not to snow under the un-technically skilled personnel man.

For example, the chemist applying for a research position could possibly snow under the personnel man who majored in social science. Yet the chemist who can make it clear to the personnel man that he invented a profitable new process for making soap will get his résumé passed on to the research V.P. A chemist who perhaps invented an even more valuable process but garbs it up in esoteric gobbledygook may get a printed rejection.

Remember, it might not be that the résumé reader, didn't want to hire someone smarter than himself. It could be that he just didn't have the time to "search for your value to the company.

DATA TO INCLUDE

What data you include in your résumé will depend on what you have done and what you want to do. How it is included will depend a great deal on the type of résumé body you choose. But before going into body styles a few general ideas can be mentioned.

Ads may help

The type of ad an employer uses to attract your attention in a newspaper may indicate the type of qualities an employer feels an applicant should have. You might try going through back issues of the paper looking for ads placed by the same company, because they may give you an idea of the outlook of the personnel manager.

Any negative data which cannot be explained simply is best left for an honest discussion at the time of the interview.

You should exclude any material from your résumé that could cast doubt in an employer's mind. If there are complex problems that are causing you difficulties in your present job your résumé is not the place to discuss them. I use a simple rule: if the problem can't be explained adequately in a single, one line sentence discard it and save the explanation for the interview.

For example, if you had cancer and have missed a great deal of time due to the sickness brought on by chemotherapy, you would not want to discuss this earlier than the interview. If a personality conflict has caused you to leave any job there is no way you can adequately cover this subject to your advantage in one sentence. Apologies do not belong in your résumé. Nor do prison records, etc. You as a résumé writer will have to make your own any decisions along these lines, but a few more guidelines are covered later in the section of this book on "Reasons for Leaving."

Body Styles

1 REVERSE TIME

The simplest form of résumé body is to list your experience beginning with your present or most recent job and work your way backwards. In this type of résumé the skills, duties and achievements are listed under the title of the job and the name of the company worked for.

This type of résumé can, in many cases, be the most efficient way of noting your past job history and working experience when the job you're applying for requires no complex skills or responsibilities. It can also be convenient if your background is rather sparse (i. e. if your a recent graduate with little or no part-time work experience.) However when complex skills need to be emphasized others résumé styles are more effective.

EXAMPLES

In the first example further below (Janet Query's) you will see we have a perfect match of résumé body to experience. Since an explanation of her duties as a secretary was not needed (The functions are basically the same in the kind of business office she is applying to.) she has chosen this simple history.

In the second example we will see another situation in which the reverse time résumé body can be used effectively (John F. Narr). Here we have a recent graduate from college whose education, rather than his experience qualifies him for the type of work he his applying for. Here the part time jobs are listed merely to give credence to the idea that he is a dependable worker who can be counted on. (In this type of résumé a short-term position in which the applicant did not get along with his employer would be tactfully omitted.

WRITING THE RÉSUMÉ BODY

The ingredients that go into a successful reverse time résumé are fairly simple.

First comes the name of the company you worked for, the address and your title and/or position in the company. (of course you could put your title first.)

Examples:

The Gouche Company, 135 Square Blvd., Barjeerling, Ohio 5401. Executive Secretary to the President. 2007 to Present

Responsibilities included all phases of office handling.....

or:

2007 to Present The Gouche Company, 135 Square Blvd., Ohio 54901. Executive Secretary to the President Responsible for all phases of office handling....

Note in the example on the next page that only one page was used.

Janet Query
13 Roscoe Street
Barjeerling, Ohio 54902   Telephone (414) 900-6487

GAL FRIDAY

Responsible office organizer with over 14 years experience in office handling and direct contact public relations. Skilled in typing (55 WPM), and shorthand.

PROFESSIONAL EXPERIENCE: (Résumé Submitted in Confidence)

The Gouche Company, 1354 Squae Blvd, Barjeerling, Ohio 54901 EXECUTIVE SECRETARY TO THE PRESIDENT.

2007 to Present: Responsibilities included all phases of office handling : Overseeing the secretarial pool (6 girls), Taking dictation for confidential meetings, Plannig the personal schedule of Mr. Gouche the company president, and acting as receptionist for the companies most important clients - handling not only personal visits but phone calls, letters and telex. Reason for desired change: Mr. Gouche's recent death.

The John Can Co., Inc., 1921 Sand Road, Barjeerling, Ohio 54901 EXECUTIVE SECRETARY

2004 to 2007: SENIOR RECEPTIONIST in this 10 member pool responsible to the executive staff of the John Can Co., Inc. Responsibilities included receptionist and secretarial duties at company board meetings. Was trusted with highly confidential company planning material. Reason for Leaving: Advancement opportunity.

2002 to 2004: SECRETARY - factory secretarial pool. Responsibilities included arranging secretarial work for in plant meetings plus numerous duties involving the factory staff.

Education:
Mitsy Tucker Secretarial School, 2000 to 2002.Graduated 4th in class of 61. Hallstead High School, 1989 to 1993, Diploma.

Personal:
Widowed Career Woman, No children, 35 years old, 5' 5-1/2", 108 lbs., Excellent Health.
Salary: Negotiable
Availability: 30 days
Excellent references available on request.

John F. Nahr
1542 Oslon Street
Yonkers, New York 10810   (921) 555-4441

R&D CHEMIST

Chemist with one year of graduate work (15credits) desiring to use his knowledge in a rewarding career position while hopefully continuing his education.

Education:

2008-2009
One year of graduate study in chemistry at the University of Dayton Ohio. Was a teaching assistant in charge of organic labs (3) and involved in studying Cr. III transition metal complexes. Carried a total of 15 credits maintaining a 3.9/4.0 index.

2004 to 2008
Earned a B.S. at Manhattan College, Bronx, New York. Transfered after freshman year from the school of Business and completed the chemistry program in 3 years. Was a member of Omega Beta Nu international social fraternity. And was editor in chief of the campus literary magazine in 1991 spring semester.

Work Experience:

May & June 2004
Temporarily employed on a part time basis as a technical advisor for the Claret Oil Company, Dayton Ohio. Was responsible for setting up a quality control lab for this oil reclaiming company. Worked until the job was completed.

John F. Nahr   Page 2

Summer 2003
Worked as a group leader at Simmon's Day Camp,
White Plains, New York.

November 1999 — June 2003
Worked week-ends at Patricia Murphy's Westchester
Candlelight Corp., Yonkers, New York. Held
various positions as host, parking attendent and
waiter.

Interests: Writing, chess, swimming, hunting
and boating

Personal: Married, 5' 9", 150 lbs., 23 years
old.

Salary: Negotiable.

Available: Immediately.

References: Excellent references available on
request.

The two variations allow for different distribution of space. The first takes up less room and is an excellent heading when you intend to show a number of positions by time period in the same company (as Janet Query did.)

The second allows you to use a bit more space if you don't have a lot to say. (John F. Narr's résumé.)

But remember the most important material in the body of any style résumé is your experience. The responsibilities you mastered should be handled in a way that shows you in a favorable light. To do this you should emphasize the talents that might appeal to your prospective employer as you explain the types of duties you performed. You should describe any special duties and responsibilities that give an indication of your value. Describe any supervisory duties and any vital tasks that are important to the functioning of the company (like handling the company payroll, or insurance policies, etc.) If you perform a task or have a function that is related to helping make the company's profits, use the companies profit figures (if readily available, publishing secret information will not impress any employer) in your résumé to demonstrate that. Describe all the machines you know how to use, and if you're a student include any part time experiences that could be relevant. Show the employer all of your experience while emphasizing what your good at.

(I you wish to go into a different field because of boredom or unease in your current profession, you might consider vocational counseling to find out what you would enjoy. A good source of this counseling might be the testing center at the nearest accredited university.)

Life does play nasty tricks on us all. It is a good idea to remember that no salesman sells to every customer he calls on. It is only the persistent salesman, who sooner or later makes the sale. If you've lost a job you must be a persistent salesman in selling yourself. Such tactics as sending out many résumés at one time[vii] ensure than no one rejection allows your hopes to be devastated. Getting hung up on the hope of getting one job is a no-no.

If you are persistent and keep at job hunting, if you don't let any rejections slow you down, you will most likely find a good job. It may take time but you will find it.

Taking a Lesser Job

Every so often a client who had lost a job would become so desperate that they asked me to include a note in their résumé that they were willing to take anything. I always refused and here are the reasons I gave for doing so:

1) If you are obviously overqualified you won't get the lesser job. A smart employer will know you'll quit at the first opportunity to work at your previously established level.
2) If you aren't obviously over qualified you will be notifying the prospective employer that you have serious doubts about your worth. Hardly a way to say, "I'm the best one for the job."
3) If you should land that lower position it may do you more personal damage then going without a job for a while would have. We evaluate ourselves in terms of our group. (There are actually a few groups in our lives, work, social, religious, which very often overlap. But here I mean the group which evaluates us a worker.) In a lesser position you quickly lose any respect your achievements have earned you in a higher one. (I know this from personal experience. I had been a research chemist with a good number of innovations and products I could claim credit for. Due to an attempt to change careers and become a full time writer I had to at one time accept a position as a factory worker. Although I could rationalize all I wanted, the fact that these factory workers treated me only as another factory worker[viii] was devastating to my college educated self-esteem. At times I began to doubt

that I could ever amount to anything better.) By not providing any of the respect your past achievements have earned you and because of that habit that groups of people have of telling you constantly in many subtle ways that you are no better than they, they can soon have you believing you can do no better. My advice is to always imply in your résumé that you will take nothing but an equal or better position.

Some further examples of the reverse time résumé follow.

Gloria A. Panati
345 Smith Court
New York, NY 10021   Telephone (503) 555-0334

KINDERGARTEN TEACHER

Dedicated, certified instructor with 15 years experience working with kindergarten children in environmentally and culturally disadvantaged areas. Fluent in both Spanish and English. Have mot recently finished a Peace Corps tour in Guatemala.

PROFESSIONAL EXPERIENCE:

March 99 to May 07
La Casa Dos Ninos, La Pinotia, Guatemala. PEACE CORPS INSTRUCTOR responsible for education and rehabilitation of orphan children of kindergarten age who were earthquake victims. Handled all phases of program planning and activities arrangement for 40 children at the orphan home school.

Reason for Leaving: Because of home-sickness decided to seek a meaningful position teaching the disadvantaged of my own country.

May 87 to March 99
Union Kinler School, Milwaukee, WI 53210. KINDERGARTEN TEACHER. Taught disadvantaged children in a special Milwaukee Cites program for the economically and culturally deprived. Headed a special program for partially deaf children. Left Milwaukee after my husband died.

December 86
North Chicago Elementary School, Chicago, IL 60601. KINDERGARTEN TEACHER. Worked with kindergarten classes of 20 to 40 in a wide field program including classroom, workshop and physical education. Husband was transferred to Milwaukee.

Gloria A. Panati   Page 2

Education:
University of Southern Illinois, B.S. Elementary Education with a minor in Physical Science.

Special Courses:
The disadvantaged Spanish speaking child a cultural outlook,
MSI Institute - Feb. 96.

Salary: Salary is less important than self-fulfillment.

Availability: Will be able to start in the fall '08 term.

Personal: 42, 5' 0", 98 lbs., Widowed, No Dependents,

                     Excellent Health.

References: Excellent References on Request.

Duane Fairchild
Route 2
Blue City, MN 56013   Telephone (643) 555-0987

Objective: ROAD WORKER

> Responsible, hardworking young man with experience in a wide variety of those tasks needed in road maintenance, plus mechanical and carpenter skills.

Professional Experience: (Résumé Submitted in Confidence)

July 98 to Present

Union Container Corp., Blue City, MN 56013, CUTTING MACHINE OPERATOR. Skills involve the measurement and set up for box cutting machinery. And the smooth operation of that machinery.

Reason for desired change: Company forecasts cutting back to a three day work week.

November 97 to May 98

Universal Tree Service, Oakridge, CA 95817, Supervisor Dan Metlow (902) 555-1224. Began as grounds-man and was promoted to foreman for this utilities pole treating company. Duties involved digging, pole preparation and protective coating application. Reasons for Leaving: Long periods away from home.

October 97 to November 97

Dawson Construction Corp., Pearl, MN 56015. CARPENTER. Roughed in houses, shingled roots, laid cement floors. Reason for Leaving: Left for higher paying position.

Duane Fairchild   Page 2

Seasonal or part-time positions:

June-September 97, Drove Truck for Dave Holden, Peas & Corn.

May-July 96 Worked on rock removal crew for Green Giant.

Education:

       Montecello High School. 1993 to 1996 Dropped out to work full time. Desire to continue for General Education Diploma.

Personal: 5' 8", 137 lbs., Single, 21 years old. No
       Dependents, Excellent Health.

Availability: Two weeks.

Salary: Negotiable.

Travel: to 50%

References: Excellent references available on request.

Jane R. Krutzman
123 Golding Circle
Indianapolis, IN 46207
Telephone (523) 597-9894

Objective: CHILDREN'S HOSPITAL STAFF NURSE

Nursing Career Woman with 7 years of professional nursing 'experience and a strong personal desire to work with children.

Professional Experience:

May 04 to Present
Department of Health & Welfare, City of Indianapolis, Indianapolis, IN 46204. STAFF NURSE PUBLIC SCHOOL SYSTEM. Responsibilities include all aspects of Public School Nursing, Prevention and detection of communicable diseases, Testing for visual and audio logical defects, Emergency First Aide, Family Health Instruction, Etc. Reason for desired change: Personal desire to take a more active part in the treatment of seriously ill children.

June 02 to May 04
Wedgewood Pediatrics Clinic, 317 Wood Ave., Bayfield, IN 60989. OFFICE NURSE AND SECRETARY TO DR. PAUL CURRY M.D. Assisted in all phases of the operation of this pediatrics office until Dr. Curry's death.

October 97 to May 02
William Coleman Hospital, 1100 W. Michigan Ave., Indianapolis, IN 46207. NURSING ASSISTANT. Worked as a nursing assistant while in nursing school to supplement student loan.

Education: Diploma, Carigan High School, 1997, B.S.

Nursing, Coleman College of Nursing, June 02.

Jane R. Krutzman   Page 2

Special Courses:

    Health problems of the Elementary School child, 2 crs. Bayfield College 2003

    Psychology of Young Burn Victims 2 crs. University of Indiana 2004

    The Dead Child and the Surviving Parent, 2 crs. University of Indiana 2004.

NURSING TECH INSTITUTE CHILDREN'S CINIC

Burn Treatment Level I, 2 hrs. Anesthesia for Children, 8 hrs.

Head Injuries, 4 hrs. Hearing Refresher, 3 hrs. Group Dynamics for Children, 3 hrs. Eye Refresher, 3 hrs.

Preparation for an Operation on an Skin Eruptions in the Small Child emotional level. Child 4 hrs. Household poisons and their NURSING EXTENSION symptoms, 15 hrs.

Shock and the Child, 13 hours The Young Rape Victim, 6 hrs.

Professional Affiliations:

United Nursing Association, Local Chairwoman, past 3 years. Volunteer
Nursing for Home bound Children. '05 to Present.

Personal: 5' 2", 132 lbs., Married, No Children, Excellent Health.

Hobbies: Swimming, Tennis, Volleyball, Hiking.

Salary: Negotiable.

Availability: 30 days

References: Excellent References Available on Request.

Fiona B. Lambert
306 Baxter Street
Sweet Water, KY 42285   Telephone (422) 555-9056

ADVERTISING SALESWOMAN

Aggressive, self-starting career woman with over 4 years of public contact advertising sales experience. Currently completing last 3 credits toward Associate degree in business.

Professional:

February 05 to Present

ADVERTISING SALESWOMAN at the Sweet Water Weekly Shopper, 421 Marion Street, Sweet Water KY 42285. Handle all phases of ad sales, from initial cold calls, thru customer contact, to sales closing. This involves customer complaints, bill collecting, copywriting, ad production, design planning and copyediting. Reason for desired change: Seeking a position with more promising personal advancement opportunities.

Education: Currently finishing last 3 credits toward my Associate degree at Columbus College of Business, Sweet Water.

Graduated third in a class of 53 from Kimberly High School.
Kimberly, Kentucky 1997.

Personal:	Divorced, No Dependents, 5' 6", 120 lbs.
Travel:	Willing to Travel.
Salary:	Negotiable.
Availability:	30 days.
References:	Excellent References available on request.

THE EXPERTISE RÉSUMÉ

As the job you are seeking becomes more complex so does the résumé you'll need to show the prospective employer you have the ability the job calls for. It is simply not enough, for example, to say: Worked at the Bubo Company for five years as General Manager of the Pillow line. If you did that you'd be breaking that very important rule I'll mention again. Don't expect the employer to look for your talents. Show him and entice him.

Most people take for granted to a certain extent their job. You may be the manager of your company for five years and be proud of that fact. But you cannot expect to simply put that fact down in one sentence and have the prospective employer comprehend magically how valuable an employee you'll be. Most of the people you send your résumé to will not know what you do better than your competition unless you tell them. And if you don't tell them they will not be inclined to waste their time giving you an interview.

The best way to show what you can do and how well you can do it is to break down the job you have performed into its basic components. In this way it is possible to show what functions you as an employee performed and give a clear picture of your duties and achievements. To break down the job effectively we must analyze the job itself.

Let's, for example, look at the manager of a retail store. The first thing a retail store must do before it can sell anything is obtain products to sell. If the manager takes part in the purchasing or ordering of goods for sale he should detail the part he plays. Does he analyze his customer's buying trends in order to see what quantities of goods need be ordered? Does he make up a purchasing budget? The idea is to tell about his skills as a purchaser.

Advertising and promotion are another important part of the retail store. Does the manager plan advertising? Does he plan promotions that he feels will help the store? Have any developments been so successful that they can be seen to have greatly helped the store?

Sales are of course very important to a retail store. Does the manager plan store sales? Does he oversee the sales force? How have the sales figures been doing over the past months? Years?

Customer relations is a direct offshoot of sales. Does the manager handle the complaints of difficult customers? How has he set store policy toward handling the complaints of customers?

Go over the various aspects that make your business run. The trick is not to overlook anything. Purchasing is obvious in retail store. But even in a service business that has relatively few purchasing requirements the ordering of those few supplies is an essential part of the business. Because you want to show talent in any area the prospective employer might expect you to work for him in, you must give as total a picture as possible of your ability.

Start by analyzing all the functions that make the company you work for an operating business. After writing these down, write down the part you played in each with emphasis on the functions you played the most important part in (and in some cases the function you feel your new employer might be most interested in.)

If you feel a function is important but that you haven't played an active enough part in it to emphasize it with a separate section on your résumé, use that function as an additional part of a larger function you can emphasize. For example: The Wendy R. Cody Résumé (to follow). An important aspect of being an ad manager is making important decisions on customer billings. Wendy's experience was with a college paper the real billing decisions were made by the school staff. But Wendy's input was the deciding factor in most cases. If Wendy had been totally in charge of the billing decisions that function would have been important enough to merit a separate section on her résumé. But she was not.

Still her involvement warrants mentioning her skills in this area so she has included it under 'Problem Solving.'

Analyze how your company operates. The following outline is a fairly good basis to start with but it is by no means totally inclusive.

AN ANALYSIS OF YOUR PART IN YOUR COMPANIES OPERATION

(It might be a good idea to have a notebook and pen available to jot ideas that arise as you read.)

1) What part do you play in the acquisition of goods your company uses in the performance of its business? This can apply to the retail store needing goods to sell, the service business which needs tools or office supplies, the manufacturing company which needs raw materials to keep up production, or even the research and development lab which needs instrumentation and scientific supplies to continue its work.

PURCHASING/SUPPLY ORDERING/ETC.

What type of materials do you purchase?
How do you evaluate the need for these supplies?
Do you have contact with sales personnel - and are you skilled in negotiating with them?
Are you responsible for checking out the ability of your suppliers to provide you with the needed quantity and quality of material?
Are you able to maintain an inventory that keeps production rolling?
Do you handle the budget for such purchases?
Have you saved the company any money as far as your handling of the purchasing is concerned?

2) What innovations have you made that add to the value of your company? In some types of business the innovations are best included under the heading of other special functions. For example, if your innovations have been in promotion, sales, or inventory control (purchasing) they would be best mentioned under those subheadings.

There are positions in which innovations are of prime importance. This would be true of the writer, editor or research scientist. In these positions innovation can be the most important factor in the résumé. In other situations such as manufacturing, innovations in machinery or production methods deserve a special heading (though they may or may not be the most important part of your résumé.)

INNOVATIONS

What innovations have you made for your company?
What was the benefit to your company?
How did it come about?
Did you originate the idea?
What is your track record for new, profitable ideas?
What is your track record for improving old, profitable ideas?
Are you able to invent or produce requested innovations on a deadline schedule?

3) What is your contribution to your company's salability? The most obvious is the role played by the company's sales force but every company employee plays at least some part in the companies being sold. Many types of people have at least some contact with their own company's sales force such as research and production people. The contact these people make to teach the salespeople about the company's products or help fill an order on time plays an important part in the company's profit making. Thus there are two meanings for the heading SALES. One is, of course, selling. The other is for describing contact with sales people in the company.

SALES (Sales Force)

What type of products are you familiar with selling?
What methods do you use to find customers? Cold Calls? Etc.?
Are you capable of determining a customer's needs?
Are you skilled in handling complaints in such a way as not to lose customers?

How many sales dollars did you bring into the company in the last month?
Quarter? Year? Or what other period was most impressive?
What has been the percentage of your sales increases over your best period?
What do you feel is the best way to represent your sales accomplishment percentage increase or dollar volume (based on the job you are looking for)?
Have there been any long-term successes in your sales career that are worth noting?
In some instances it can be worthwhile to describe your selling success in terms of your product knowledge (i.e. how your special knowledge helped you make sales.) This can be helpful in fields like computer or chemical sales.

SALES (Working with the Sales Force)

What type of contact do you have with the company sales force?
Do you work with them regularly to ensure that the customer's needs are being met?
Do you contact customers to work out their exact needs?
Can you communicate to sales personnel important technical data and information they need to be effective?

Do you have an effective communication system with the sales team ensuring your knowledge or priorities? (I.e. The manufacturing director has to know how much product to make next month.)
Do you plan your work according to the sales force's prediction of future sales?
Do you work with sales to get information needed for long-term decisions?

4) What part do you play in company advertising? Everybody advertises at least in the way of making their company known to the people they work with. Some, like salesmen, may advertise by word of mouth only. Yet others are responsible for using whatever media is available to them. Not everyone will have had experience in advertising or working with advertising. You may

not need to. But if advertising is important in your job - you must show your ability in it.

ADVERTISING:

What types of accounts or what types of products do you do advertising for?
What types of media do you use or are you familiar with?
How often or what is the extent of your use of these media?
Do you create the ads yourself?
How do you measure the response to your advertising?
Do you plan the advertising budget?
Do you handle the advertising for special sales?
Do you have skills in graphics, photography, filmmaking or any other art that is of use in advertising?

5) Do you take active part in the promotion of your company?
Promotion is directly related to advertising in many ways, but here, I'm referring to the ways of promoting the company's goods and services outside of media advertising.

PROMOTION

Do you plan sales promotions?
Do you plan and/or set up store displays?
Do you promote the company by making speeches?
Do you arrange for promotional tours?
Do you set up or are you involved in trade shows for dealers?
Do you work with manufacturing representatives?
Do you work with marketing personnel advising them about your company's products or services?
Do you attend business meetings, luncheons, and dinners or attend conventions to promote your company?
Do you take the responsibility for the financial planning of such promotions?

6) Do you take an active part in analyzing the credit responsibility of your company's customers? Or your own company's credit?

CREDIT

Are you familiar with your company's collection procedures and have you had a part in forming them?
Have you handled or taken measures on tardy accounts?
Are you responsible in any way for your own company's credit rating?
Are you able to handle discrepancies, handle billing errors, and deal with suppliers in such cases in a manner favorable to your company?

7) Are you responsible for the supervision of others?
The ability to supervise and train others is an important asset to any executive. Because most executives do supervise others it is an important part of the managerial résumé. If you supervise others in any way you should take advantage of the prestige supervision affords you.

SUPERVISORY

How many people have you supervised? (If you supervise foremen or managers you would also list how many people each was responsible for.)
Have you negotiated with unions?
Do you have knowledge of fair employment practices?
Have you increased your employee's production rate? How?
Have you made your production or sales staff or whatever more efficient by reorganizing the use of manpower?
Have you interviewed prospective employees and made hiring decisions?
Have you determined salary increases?
Have you taken disciplinary action in regards to misconduct by employees under you? Have you done this fairly?
(Note: Although some people like to use the term "Responsible for Hiring and Firing" I don't feel the term firing is in good taste. It is overly simple and does not indicate the use of judgment on the part of supervisor. Ironically it seemed to be favored by those who were unemployed.)

Do your employees respect you? Do they enjoy working for you?
Have you the ability to look at your employee's situation from their point of view? Are you familiar with OSHA, ERISA, etc.? (If you are not sure everyone will understand an abbreviation: spell it out.)

8) Do you handle any of the general business operations of your company?
This is of course a very general heading, which allows you to include responsibilities not covered under other headings. And also activities you are only partially responsible for.

GENERAL BUSINESS

Are there any functions you perform that although they don't merit a separate heading would merit a listing under general business because they are essential to the company?
Do you handle some of your department's bookkeeping?
(Here in the bookkeeping area it is well to distinguish those who simply perform a few bookkeeping functions from accountants whose sole duty to the company is handling the books. An accountant might have a separate section solely on accounting or bookkeeping.) Do you make up work schedules? Do you handle dispatching? Do you handle payroll? Are you responsible for time cards? Are you ordering or purchasing for the company but don't feel these require a separate section?

9) Do you have other skills you feel require a heading?
As was mentioned, in no way is the above list meant to be totally inclusive. There are endless possibilities for headings. You, because you know yourself, are in a better position to distinguish what is most important as far as your skills go. Newspaper ads can be a source of subjects for the résumé body as well as for the headings. The needs of the company you are applying to, listed in ads or other sources make good headings. For example, if an ad calls for someone skilled in troubleshooting you could have

a heading called TROUBLESHOOTING and list your abilities under that heading.

A FEW MORE EXAMPLES OF FUNCTIONING HEADLINES FOLLOW WITH SOME ADDITIONAL OBSERVATIONS AND RULES.

INTERCOMPANY COMMUNICATONS: If you play an important part in a company function such as the transfer of information throughout your company you might list your skills under a heading such as this.

INVENTORY ANALYSIS: Here is an example of how a part of a larger function (Purchasing) may be used as a separate section. This may be because the applicant wishes to divide his function further to make it more easily understood. Or because the applicant only performs this part of the larger function.

RAW MATERIAL ANALYSIS: Here is another part of that larger function (Purchasing). But is it? Research & Development people and certain production personnel may or may not have more than a minor say in company purchases outside of their department. Even if they do not control materials outside their department, they still may be responsible for evaluating the materials they come in contact with. A school janitor may be required to keep supplies on hand, and the person who gets the janitor's job may be the one to mention their ability to order supplies. Don't think of your functions merely in terms of your major functions. You should take the initiative to best describe what you do and can do in terms of meeting an employer's needs.

EXPANSION PLANNING: If you've taken an active part in the planning of your company's growth this certainly deserves a heading. It is somewhat similar to the next example.

MANUFACTURING: If you've made innovations in a variety of departments you might consider listing each separately under the title of the department.

PRODUCTION MANAGEMENT: Titles must e flexible also. A wide range of duties in all phases of production would be better titled PRODUCTION MANAGEMENT than GENERAL BUSINESS. Or use your own title as long as you can explain it.

ANYTHING: Anything that you wish to emphasize can be used as a heading for the body of your expertise résumé. The examples will give you some further ideas. But the basic tenet is after analyzing what your company does explain what you do in it and use the titles so as to best explain it.

SOME ADDITIONAL RULES ON LISTING YOUR FUNCTIONS

The total of the functions you list should give a complete and accurate list of all you are expert at doing. The following rules will help you create your list successfully.

- List functions once and only once. There is no point or benefit in being redundant in a résumé.
- List functions in the most logical order possible. The functions may be interconnected and difficult to give an order to. But you should try to make it as easy as possible for the prospective employer to understand what you do. The most logical order is based on how your company operates (ex. purchasing - innovation - manufacturing - goods - advertising/promotion - sales.) Simply put down your functions in the order of the steps your company takes to do business.
- If you can break down your functions into smaller self-sufficient areas do so. (I.e. Purchasing: = Budget Planning, Raw Material Evaluation, Buyer-Salesman Contact, etc. A purchasing agent should not list simply purchasing.)

Examples:

Wendy R. Codi Home Address:
235 Bleeker St. 800 High St.
North Ridge, CA 90956 Brandyville, CA 90654
(516) 555-3309 (516) 555-9934

ADVERTISING SALES

Profit-oriented self-starter with a very successful Record as Ad Manager of Bright College's WEEKLY PHOENIX, desiring to combine sales, supervisory, problem solving and decision making ability with a journalism degree to effect a highly profitable career position.

AREAS OF EXPERIENCE:

With the WEEKLY PHOENIX, Bright College's student paper was Ad Manager controlling $1400 to $1800 dollars per week in advertising revenue. Ad Manager Fall 2008 and Spring 2008. Ad Sales Representative - Spring 2007.

SALES: Responsible for 3 paid sales staff members and 2 to 3 voluntary sales people. Have increased revenue from last year.

SUPERVISORY: In addition to sales promotion am responsible for payroll and commission determinations.

PROBLEM SOLVING: Responsible for determining and correcting customer problems concerning advertisements. Expert in calming irate customers and arranging for payments on disputed ads. Although not directly responsible for billing my decisions have been the one followed through on.

PRODUCTION: Responsible for advertising deadlines. Total ad determination. Placement of ads (working with the design editor) and final proofreading.

OTHER WORK EXPERIENCE: Has included mail order department work and waitressing. Details upon request.

Education: Bright College, B.S. May 2008 Journalism/Advertising and Public Relations with emphasis on advertising and public relations.

Personal: Single, 5' 4", 110 lbs., Born 5/16/1985. Excellent Health. From a small community - raised on a farm. Have traveled all over the U.S., Europe and South America.

Activities: Vice-President of Sigma Delta Chi/Society for Professional Journalists. Former Senator and presently assembly person for Bright College's Student Association.

Hobbies: Riding, Tennis, Golf, Skiing, Swiming
Salary: Negotiable.
Travel: Willing to travel.
Relocation: Willing to Relocate.
References: Excellent references on request.

Thomas B. Gibbs
45 North Hayland
Omar, Nebraska 98895   (846) 895-0987

PERSONNEL MANAGER

Supervisor with 24 years experience as a foreman and 4 years as a union business representative, expert in labor relations, union negotiations and handling the requirements of OSHA, ERISA and EEO, desiring a challenging management career.

AREAS OF PROFESSIONAL EXPERTISE:

1995 to Present, Business Representative for local 234 of the United Steel Mill Workers of America. Would like to change do to the fact that professional growth is limited and there is limited security in a politically appointed position.

- Union Negotiations: Have become skilled as a negotiator working out contracts and effecting settlements between unions and management.
- Inter-Union Bargaining: Expert in inter-union negotiations between striking unions.
- Placement: Have acted as union job dispatcher analyzing personnel and choosing the best suited people for the job in question.

1971 to 1995 Supervisory:, FOREMAN, The Kilman Steel Company, Baltimore, MD. Was rapidly promoted in this company. As foreman was directly responsible for 24 employees in the pouring room. Handled all aspects of employee problems, etc.

Reason for Leaving: Had been so involved in union activities that taking on a full time position seemed the thing to do.

Thomas B. Gibbs   Page 2
45 North Hayland
Omar, Nebraska 98895   (846) 895-0987

Education:

    Delano Roosevelt High School.
    1968 to 1971, General Diploma.

Personal:

    Married
    56 years old
    6' 0", 195 lbs.
    2 children
    Good Health.

Hobbies: Sailing, skiing, fishing.

Salary: Negotiable.

Availability: 30 days.

References: Excellent references available on request.

John J. Fredrickson
1245 Algoma Place
Marketsville, NH 10135   (413) 555-9809

Objective: SALES REPRESENTATIVE

Aggressive, self-starting junior buyer with over $3 million in yearly purchasing responsibility for a leading manufacturer of children's toys, desiring to combine knowledge of production & manufacturing, continuing education, and problem solving ability toward implementing a profitable career in sales with long term management goals.

PROFESSIONAL EXPERIENCE: (Résumé Submitted in Confidence)

Mairbell Toy Company, 1290 Jefferson Road, Bagston, NH 10137

JUNIOR BUYER and Inventory Control Manager for the Doll and Doll Clothing units of this toy company. Joined the company in 2001 and was promoted to Junior Buyer after the first year on the job.

EXPERTISE:

- INVENTORY CONTROL: Activities involve the continuous inter-communication between sales and manufacturing in order to predict future sales trends and insure material supplies that will guarantee manufacturing productivity.

- BUYER-SALESMAN CONTACT: As buyer of both plastic raw materials and screen printed fabric - have a wide range of experience in sales and manufacturing representative contact with regards to the determination of prices and the availability of the necessary raw materials.

- PURCHASING: Have become skilled not only in material evaluation but in evaluating the production capabilities of possible new suppliers. Have developed an operative computer program for cost analysis of purchased raw material.

- INNOVATIONS: Have developed in conjunction with the data processing center an automatic raw material reordering schedule based on the invoices of sales, production supply inventory, and manufactured product to date. This has been highly effective in preventing down time on the production line.

OTHER WORK EXPERIENCE:

WAITER, Khal's Whitestone House Restaurant, Markey City, NH 10133 Worked part time while attending Olin University earning 100% of tuition.

Education: Olin University, 1997 to 2001, B.B.A. Graduated Cum Laude.

Personal: 6' 3", 198 lbs., Excellent Health, Married, No Children

Salary Negotiable, Willing to Travel and Relocate, Available in 30 days,

Excellent References available on request.

Douglas Wayfield
1324 Fir Street
Greenfield, IL 30808   Telephone
(996) 456-2314

HEAD HUNTER

Skilled communicator with 6 years of intense local experience in making successful placements for the Illinois Job Service, desiring to combine experience and knowledge in implementing a profitable career in Management Consulting.

PROFESSIONAL: (Résumé Submitted in Confidence)

Over the past 6 years I have been an active recruiter in this area for the Illinois Job Service.

I. FUNDAMENTAL KNOWLEDGE OF LOCAL BUSINESS STRUCTURES: Including: Retail Management, Hospital and Health Care, Factory Work, Production & Planning Management, Printing, Sales (all areas from door-to-door to Industrial Sales Management), Computer Specialization, Public Relations, Secretarial, Community Management, Artistic, Teaching, and Specialized Cases.

II. RAPPORT: Have developed rapport with local employers and with employees that I have placed. This provides a wide range of personal contacts in this area that can be drawn upon.

RELATED SKILLS:

As a project for a graduate level course in Developmental Psychology have developed a number of testing mediums for determining an individual's compatibility with his work environment. These have proven highly successful in finding long-term employment for workers who have had a difficult time finding employment due to erratic work records.

Have published three papers in the field:
- I. "Your Skills are Your Assets" June 82 issue of Management Magazine.
- II. "Hire From the Outside or Promote From Within?" July 81, Ibid.
- III. "When an Employee Says he is Quitting" December 79, Ibid.

And am currently working on another.

Education

B.S. from Glintondale College, Major Psychology, Minor Sociology.

Graduate Extension Course Glintondale Professional Counseling and Developmental Psychology.

Personal:	5' 6", 130 lbs., Married, 3 Children,
	Excellent Health.
Availability:	30 days.
Travel:	Limited Travel.
Salary:	Negotiable.

Excellent References on request.

Lee Sheridan
1335 North View Terrace
White Plains, NY 10905   Telephone (590) 555-9888

Objective: MANAGEMENT EXECUTIVE

Widely experienced military officer desiring to combine vast executive military experience with M.B.A. knowledge in the organization of a profitable civilian business career.

PROFESSIONAL:

CAPTAIN: U.S. Army, currently Assistant Professor of Military Science at White Plains College, Military executive experience has included; Mechanized Infantry Company Commander, Assistant Training and Operations Officer, and Motor Officer. (2003 to Present.)

MANAGEMENT: Management duties have included a wide area of subjects from the organization of training programs to the supervision and maintenance of over 150 vehicles. Expert in the organization and planning of entire detailed programs from kitchen staffing to field training plans. Experienced in budget planning, physical security, safety and other areas.

SUPERVISORY: Responsibility has involved commanding up to 187 men. Experienced in all phases of personnel motivation and problem solving. Activities included promotions, disciplinary actions, solving personal problems and other necessary functions to insure the smooth operation of the unit.

COMMUNICATION SKILLS: Actively involved in communication as Assistant Professor of Military Science at White Plains College. Have traveled for the army giving promotional talks at High Schools.

Detailed history of military duty will be furnished on request.

Education:

Newly High School, Newly, New York, College Prep, 1994 - 1998, graduate.

University of Columbus Ohio, 1998 — 1999 Political Science/English, B.A.

New York University, 2007 - 2009, will receive M.B.A. in December 2009.

Personal: Single 5' 10", 198 lbs. Excellent Health.

Hobbies: Skiing, Boating, Skin-diving.

Available: 90 days.
Salary: Negotiable.
Travel: Willing to travel to 80%.

Excellent references available on request.

Web E. Daniels
809 Parrot St.
Baltimore, MD 21296   415-555-4041

Business Address
Baltimore Water Control Bureau
110 Down St.
Baltimore, MD 21279   415-555-9896

Objective: ENVIROMENTAL SYSTEMS RESEARCH

Dedicated environmentalist with a M.S. in environmental engineering and experience in both industry and government funded graduate level research projects desiring a rewarding career in the developmental area of environmental systems research.

SOME HIGHLIGHTS OF PROFESSIONAL EXPERIENCE:

Currently a GROUP LEADER in the Environmental Engineering Division of the Baltimore Water Control Bureau, responsible for the direct operation of the environmental waste systems analysis unit. (Résumé Submitted in Confidence.)

- INNOVATIONS: Innovations include a highly efficient system of random waste water sampling for foundry out-flow. Numerous papers in the field (please see publications) and a number of computerized programs for the analysis of collected sample data.

- PROGRAM DEVELOPMENT: Skilled in the development and follow-through in all areas involved in an environmental control operation. In addition to those necessary functions such as budget forecast, cost planning and field lab work.

Web E. Daniels   Page 2

- o SUPERVISION: Currently responsible for a working environmental lab staff of six, two Senior Scientists, two Junior Scientists and two Technicians. Have become skilled in the directing and training of employees in both lab and field. Have also promoted a high level of employee satisfaction in the work.

PROFESSIONAL HISTORY: (Résumé Submitted in Confidence)

August 1979 to Present:

GROUP LEADER, Baltimore Water Control Bureau. (Outlined above) Reason for desired change: Would like the opportunity to partake in the developmental areas of environmental protection.

Summer 1997 to 1998

WASTE PROCESSING ENGINEER'S ASSISTANT, Kilman Steel Corporation (government funded) summer position after senior year in college and after first year in graduate school. Was included as part of Master's research project. Project related to the environmental impact assessment of the new Kilman Steel Mill on the Mayopac River.

Web E. Daniels Résumé page 2

Education:

B.S. Baltimore State University, Chemistry, 1993 - 1997. Graduated 5th in class of 40. Magna Cum Laude.

M.S. Baltimore State University, Environmental Engineering, 1997 to 1979. Magna Cum Laude

July 1997 to May 1979, Graduate Research Assistant with Dr. David Milton Clyde. Government environmental impact assessment grant.

SPECIAL EDUCATION:

> Data Base Concepts. B.S.U. 1979 Special Problems in Computer Science, B.S.U. 1980.
>
> Environmental Scientists Symposium at Rivershot: 1997, 1998, 1979, 1980 & 1981.

PUBLICATIONS:

Clyde, D. M. and Daniels, W.E. "The Systematic Collection of Random Samples for Waste Water Treatment Analysis." ENVIRONMENTAL SYSTEMS, Vol. 22, No. 15, August 3, 1998, pages 1225-1227.

Clyde, D.M. and Daniels, W.E. "Analysis of Heavy Metal Systems by Atomic Absorption in the little Kilman River." ENVIRONMENTAL SYSTEMS, Vol. 23, No. 17, September 12, 1995, pages 2047 - 2048.

Daniels, W.E. "Our Fragile River" Sunday Scene Magazine of the Baltimore Gazette, June 5, 1981, pages 1, 3 - 6.

PROFESSIONAL ORGANIZATIONS:

Member of the Brotherhood of Professional Environmental Engineers.

Personal: 26, Married, 5' 8", 140 lbs., 3 children, Excellent Health.

Hobbies: Boating, fishing, bowling, painting, and golf.

Salary: Negotiable.

Travel: 40%.

Availability: 30 days.

References: Excellent references available on request.

REASON FOR LEAVING: IS JUST AS IMPORTANT IN THE EXPERTISE RÉSUMÉ AS IT IS IN THE REVERSE TIME RÉSUMÉ and for the same reasons. The added dimension (you'll note from the examples) is that in cases where advancement is the reason for wanting a change in position it can neatly be mentioned in the heading and left out of the body of the résumé.

INGREDIENTS TO COMPLETE THE PACKAGE:

In any type of résumé certain information is essential, and other information has a traditional role. Since only the employer can tell you what is essential to him a good amount of the traditional must be included as well. Information about your personal life and hobbies, the answers to questions as to whether you'll travel or not should be looked at as just an easy way to give a bit of valuable but not selling information about you.

1) Personal Information: (This is not absolutely necessary but may influence employers, so consider carefully what effect the information may have on the potential employer to make your decision whether or not to include it.)

Age: Leaving out your age may make it look like you are trying to hide it. The best thing to do with age is assert that you have the experience to go with it. Aggressive enthusiasm can overcome many of the "He's too old" thoughts an employer might have. (It may be illegal to discriminate because of age but that does not mean employers will not do it.[ix])

Weight: Feel free to write lbs. instead of pounds. Or leave this out.

Height: 5' 6", is more conservative of valuable space than 5 feet 6 inches. But this isn't essential either.

Married, Single, Divorced, Etc: In some cases

this can be essential. An employer might have doubts about hiring a woman whose husband's job might force her to move in the future. Especially if an expensive training period is involved. Always think about what concerns an employer may have and try to answer them.

Number of Children and Other Dependents: The responsibility of family life can work for or against you. If you are a married male telling that to an employer can assure him that you are a responsible family man. If unmarried it can give the employer vague fears you will take off from work when your child becomes ill.

Health: If it is excellent say so. Good health means you can work but that your health leaves something to be desired. No other reply is suggested.

2) Hobbies: Few people have hobbies directly related to their work. But by showing you have hobbies, you add further dimension to your self-portrait. Who knows maybe the employer has the very same ones. (Once at an interview for some stupid reason, I started to put down bow hunting for deer [a sport I had never tried but since have tried come to respect] by saying I couldn't see sitting in a tree all day waiting for a deer to come by. It turned out the fellow I was talking to loved bow hunting and I lost the job.]

3) References: After reading every available book in the field on résumé writing I came to the conclusion that most writer's feel the references should not be named on the résumé. The reasoning behind this idea is that there is a danger the employer might contact your references before contacting you. I am a little skeptical of this. The only feedback I have gotten in this area is from customers who used references on the résumé, whose references WERE contacted BEFORE they were, and who got the jobs they wanted. Still, that old rule, "Don't gamble if you can't afford to lose" does help the "no references on the résumé" rule make sense. And this is because when you include your references on you résumé you give up control of how and when they will be

contacted. Your references may not always be in moods that will be beneficial to you when your prospective employer calls. Or they may be so busy as to not give you the reference you deserve. The worst possibility of giving up control of who contacts your references is that they will be over-contacted. If too many personnel managers inundate your references with calls about you, your reference could become your enemies. And because I advocate sending out many, many résumés this does become a danger. I suggest therefore that on your résumé you state simply: Excellent references available on request.

4) Salary: Never mention a dollar figure in your résumé unless you are writing a special résumé for a specific company. You should have an idea of what you'd like to make but it is unwise to limit yourself to a dollar figure. Many companies have health benefits and pension plans, etc. that can make a lower salary very attractive. The word "Negotiable" invites the company to tell you what it has to offer.[x]

5) Travel: Are you willing to travel as part of your job. Obviously many sales people must do this, but other positions may require you to travel away from home. The following scale gives the percent travel (approximate) for different numbers of days.

2 days - 30%
3 days - 43%
4 days - 60%
5 days - 72%
6 days - 88%
7 days - 100%

The percentages usually indicate an average over a year's time. If you wish to be away no more than a specific number of days each week you should indicate the specific number. 2 days per week, 3 days per week, etc.

Availability: One important question your employer to be will have is: when will you be able to start working? If you are unemployed it is just as okay to put down immediately as any other available date. But if you are employed the amount of time you should give your old employer as notice depends on the responsibilities of your job. What you don't want to do is give your prospective new employer the idea you will leave him out on a limb. He will very often judge how you will treat him by how you treated your past employers. For the skilled and unskilled worker two weeks is plenty of time. But if you are an executive a 30 day notice can give the impression that you care enough about your employer to tie up loose ends and also says a little about your value to the company. But this does not mean you should act foolishly. If your present company has a tendency to boot people out the day they give notice[xi]--giving such notice is not advised. But you should still put 30 days in your résumé. At the interview explain there may be a chance you'd be available sooner. Be flexible; don't let a good opportunity pass you by because you couldn't be available to your new employer by a certain date due to some fixed idea about notice. When rushed, however, double check the company before you take the job.

THE ACCOMPLISHMENT RÉSUMÉ

   One way to prepare your résumé is to list on it the accomplishments that detail your special skills in action.

   The accomplishment résumé can be a form unto itself as in the first example to follow. Or accomplishments can be added to an expertise or reverse-time résumé.

If you feel that your accomplishments can help you get a job: use them. However you should note that in its pure form the accomplishment résumé must be directed at a very precise audience. Because you are using your accomplishments to tell of your expertise the reader must know enough about your area of expertise to be able to appreciate your accomplishments.

   The accomplishment résumé should not be used alone to prove your innovative ability if you are changing fields of employment. In that case you should add achievements to an expertise or reverse-time résumé, giving ample proof that you will be able to carry over your inventive ability into your new field.

In longer résumés, accomplishments can be used to highlight the résumé and back up claims made in the heading.

BALANCE

Balance is achieved in your résumé when your design, your positioning of type, gives a good impression. The opposite of balance is disorder.

In both the single and multi-page résumé balance is achieved through consistency.

1) Margins top bottom and left should be similar on every page.

2) Use indentations with style in mind: Note how in the Elkstone résumé the word "Telephone" on page 1 and "Page" on page 2 are lined up.

James K. Elkstone
3405 West Yonkers
Helena, MT 59643   Telephone (113) 555-0987

PRODUCTION INSTRUMENTATION SPECIALIST

Professional with 20 years experience in all phases of the installation and calibration of production instruments.

PROFESSIONAL: (Résumé Submitted in Confidence)

1998 to Present
Mountain Carton Company, Inc. Helena, MT 59643
Production Instrumentation Specialist

History: Master Mechanic & Electrician, Maintenance Supervisor, Apprentice Electrician, Production Worker.

ACCOMPLISHMENTS:
- Supervised the installation of all plant and production equipment in the new Point Road facility.
- Devised a numerical key-code system which greatly enhanced installation efficiency.
- Personally directed the installation of all boiler systems for the new plant and set up maintenance programs for them.
- Set up the carton folding machines and the established the necessary facilities upgrade with the architect and construction company's electrical engineering consultant.
- Designed an air-flow control unit for the coal fired boilers that is highly efficient when feeding waste cartons.
- Designed a heat recycling system on the waxed carton sealer which saves 10 - 20% yearly in plant heating costs.
- Redesigned the paper feeders for the large carton folders.
- Oversaw the installation of all new jet printing equipment for specialty boxes.
- Evaluated the capabilities of all available stapling machines with the General Production Manager and made suggestions for those adjustments needed.

James K. Elkstone   Page 2

- Have worked with the purchasing department in establishing a maintenance cost-analysis system in which quick wearing pieces of production equipment may be purchased at the best possible price.
- Set up newly purchased stapling machines and established air pressure controls for even staple driving.
- Redesigned the paper cutting calibration controls to allow for more consistently accurate cutting.

Military: Army, 1996 - 1998, Honorable Discharge

Education: Diploma, Helena High School, 1992 – 1996 Helena Technical Extension: Electronics 1998 – 2002 Industrial Mechanics 2002 - 2005

Company Sponsored Courses:
- Air Pressure & Equipment 1999
- Boiler Installation 1997
- Maintenance Cost Analysis, 2001
- Mechanical & Electrical Maintenance, 1998 - 2000.
- Packaging Theory, 1998
- Paper Cutters 1996
- Plant Heating, 1999 - 2000
- Printing Machine Repair, 1997
- Production Computerization 1997

Personal: Divorced 40 years old 5' 11"
                       187 lbs. Good Health

Salary: Negotiable. Willing to Travel. Willing to Relocate

Hobbies: Tennis, Sky Diving[xii], Swimming

Availability: 30 days

References: Excellent References Available on Request.

SOME FINAL NOTES ON YOUR RÉSUMÉ AND YOUR EXPERIENCE

Remember the most important material in the body of any style résumé is your experience. The responsibilities you mastered should be handled in a way that shows you in a favorable light. To do this you should emphasize the talents that might appeal to your prospective employer as you explain the types of duties you performed. You should describe any special duties and responsibilities that give an indication of your value. Describe any supervisory duties and any vital tasks that are important to the functioning of the company (like handling the company payroll, or insurance policies, etc.) If you perform a task or have a function that is related to helping make the company's profits, use the companies profit figures in your résumé to demonstrate that. (If freely available: publishing secret information will not impress any employer.) Describe all the machines you know how to use and if you're a student include any part time experiences that could be relevant. Show the employer all of your experience while emphasizing what your good at. Although the employer will be looking for the talents he needs in your résumé don't expect him to search between the lines for them.

REASON FOR LEAVING

In journalism, a good story is when where the reader has no questions when the story is done. We, however, want to leave the employer with questions that will make him wish to interview us.

What we don't want to do is leave the employer with any unnecessary questions of a negative variety. We don't want to leave any vague doubts in the prospective employer's mind about us as prospective employees. Leaving such doubts could be a hindrance to our getting an interview.

If we include the reasons why we left previous jobs or why we want to leave our present job, this can be an added point in our favor. It can help build the employer's belief that we are worth taking the time to interview.

In giving our reasons for leaving we should be as honest as possible. Employers realize that at times euphemisms are necessary. Just don't make your euphemisms amount to direct lies. Lies in résumés do have a habit of catching up to you. (I'm referring here to deliberate falsehoods concerning verifiable facts. If you were fired to stealing and you say you quit for a better job, that is a lie. I you say you can successfully handle a sales force and your ex-supervisor says you can't, that is a difference of opinion - not a lie, and the rule is your supervisor is wrong.)

But it would not be wise to jeopardize a new job before you even start it by lying on your résumé.

This does not mean that your ex-employer's reason for firing you (if that was the case) is the only one you can mention. This is your résumé and it is your side of the story that is important. But be brief. If your side of the story requires considerable time to explain, the interview, not your résumé, is the place to explain it.

Whenever you can give a plausible reason for leaving on your résumé do so. One very popular reason that fits almost any situation except when you are currently unemployed is: Personal and Professional Growth.

Euphemisms can be helpful in many instances, especially when one is tempted to use negative terms about one's employer or supervisors. Although quite a few clients have told me they quit because their boss was a crook I have never felt that that was the type of statement that helps a prospective employer's view of you. It can give the idea that you are a complainer or a sorehead who has to put the blame on someone else. The situation can be handled in other ways. One résumé writer who's description of her supervisor at her kindest moment was to refer to her as a female dog described her reason for leaving euphemistically as, "Seeking a position with more promising personal advancement opportunities."

If your boss is the type of crook that has been arrested and has had his name in the papers and on television for the offense, then by all means say so. Euphemisms are not necessary when certain knowledge is available for all. (Unless of course you plan on working for another crook.)

It may interest you to know that there is an exception to the laws of civil libel called privileged communication. What it means is that if a prospective employer asks one of your old employers for a reference and the employer says you were a bum you may not be able to sue for libel because it was a privileged communication. (Imagine what would happen if ex-employees could sue bosses who gave them bad references.)

Since fair is fair the opposite is also true. If you say something bad about your employer: using it as a reason for leaving in your résumé then it too might be considered a privileged communication and you might not be successfully sued for libel. The keyword is successfully. You can be sued for almost anything. The person suing might not win but could sue. If you did put negative information concerning your past employer in your résumé you'd better make sure either you can prove it is true or you are sending it out only as needed to obtain a job. (i.e. it is a privileged communication.). If a judge or jury could be convinced you were sending out libelous information (legally libelous would mean false information or
true information you can't prove to be true. In a libel case the burden of proof is on the publisher of the libelous words.)only to cause your ex-boss embarrassment you could be in trouble.

And again I suggest you leave out negative things altogether.

I'd also like to make one last point about including reasons for leaving in our résumé. YOU ARE WRITING A COMPETITIVE RÉSUMÉ. If your competition puts down a plausible reason for leaving and you don't have you, and the employer has time for only one interview, your lack of a reason may hurt you.

IF YOU'VE BEEN FIRED

Many people who have been fired from a job suffer from a devastating lack of self-confidence. This lack of self-confidence can be fatal to your job finding ability.

It is important to realize, if you've been fired, that this lack of confidence can exist in you. Even if you think you feel only anger, the idea that you are not in control of your situation can make you feel terribly impotent. All to often people lose jobs because of communication problems or personality conflicts. The basis for these two types of problems can often be so subtle that rather than understanding them we end up with vague fears that the world is against us.

The fact that you have been fired from a job does not make you a failure as a human being, even if you aren't a young man anymore. It is an unfortunate fact of life that employers do turn out employees after 20 years of loyal service. So being fired does not make any person a failure. It cannot remove the talents that will make you of value to other employers. The problem is that we must evaluate the truth of our situation. This is often not an easy task.

The thing that must be decided is whether you wish to stay in the same field. Did the learning experience of being fired give you the knowledge you need to be successful in similar position with another company, or if you wish to try something new? Once you decide that you just have to go out and find that new job. a good cover letter, résumé combination will help you not matter what you chose.

PART TWO: THE COVER LETTER

THE IDEA

Your résumé is your advertisement. It is the formal selling item in your product presentation on paper. The cover letter is by comparison only an accessory or an adjunct. But there is very good reason for it.

Résumés are bulk selling tools for the most part. They are meant to be sent out to numerous employers so that you may find the one or ones who have a need for your skills. Now you could send your résumés out by themselves, but if you do you may be selling yourself short.

You should always keep in mind that it will be a person who will hire you. And it is a social reality that people will pay a lot more attention to us when we treat them as persons. This fact is borne out by the success of computer printed advertising addressed to specific individuals rather than "Occupant." We must pay some attention to the individual if we wish them to pay some attention to us.

In the job hunt we must be aware of the personal end of the selling problem. The cover letter is a combination of social grace and a tool. It is a social grace because it recognizes the individual in a polite manner. It is a tool because it captures the attention of the employer and focuses it on the product, us.

SOME PRACTICAL CONSIDERATIONS FOR THE COVER LETTER

The main reason that a résumé was often bulk printed in the past was that it contains a good deal of information that must be presented accurately each time. To send out individually typed résumés on the old fashioned typewriter was a monumental task. To type one good résumé, proofread it, make corrections and then print up hundreds of copies was far more practical. Nowadays we can keep our resume on a computer and tweak it whenever we feel like it, printing as we need to. Offset printing still does present a nice looking resume, and since changes often lead to typographical errors I recommend you get one good proofread copy and use it without revising. The choice of using offset or other printing or not is yours. Today, however, many can duplicate the qualities that use to be exclusive to offset printing with a computer and quality printer on carefully selected paper.[xiii]

With the cover letter, however, you will be sending out individual copies. So the best way to keep down the possibility of error is to keep the sections you plan on changing from letter to letter as short as possible. Write carefully, be brief, then put each aside for a while to get some distance from your thoughts[xiv], before proofreading carefully.

STARTING ON THE RIGHT FOOT - RESEARCHING THE COMPANY AND THE PERSON YOU APPLY TO.

It is flattering to have someone take the time and trouble to find out who you are. It can even be flattering when these people obviously want something because it is a measure of our prestige that they have to go through us to get what they want.

You can use flattery as a tool in your job hunt by taking a little extra time to research the company you are applying to and the individual your résumé will be read by. This research will give you a decided advantage over those who don't do it.

The first step in researching any company used to be to talk to one of the reference librarians at your local library. Today many searches can be done online through companies like Google and Yahoo. (I recommend a number of search engines as they will turn up different info sometimes.) However, unless you are a pro at internet searches I still recommend you visit an expert—your local reference librarian. They are experts in research and are paid to help you. In addition to the internet they might suggest reference books such as Standard and Poor's Directory of American Corporations, and others, which might contain the names of the officers of the company. They might also direct you to the telephone books which contain names and phone numbers you won't be asked to pay for[xv]. If need be you can call the receptionist at the company you wish to apply to and ask her the name and title of the person (with correct spelling) you should address your application to.

Because the reference librarian can be a big help to you in your job hunt, it might pay to cultivate a friendship. The librarian will always be up to date on the latest reference works giving employment in your field.

This kind of job research is important. Most of the jobs filled are not listed in advertisements or on the local job service (DO GO THERE AND REGISTER) message board[xvi]. I strongly suggest that you locate any and every company that has the kind of job that you want and send a résumé and cover letter to an individual (not Personnel Office) that you've found through your research. Set realistic a goal for yourself, say ten mailings a day on days you don't have interviews and three on days you do. (No, don't stop sending out résumés until you get a job.)
THE BASIC COMPONENTS OF YOUR COVER LETTER - WHAT TO MENTION

The following are essential ingredients that must be included in your cover letter.

THE RÉSUMÉ: The idea of your cover letter is to introduce your résumé. So you must say, "Here is my résumé," in some way or another.

THE COMPANY: You should prove you know something about the company you are applying to - and that you have done your homework. By separating yourself from the swarms of applicants who waste an employer's time by showing they know nothing about his business, you can gain more interest in your application.

THE INTERVIEW: You must mention in your letter that you are sending your résumé along in the hopes of obtaining a job interview. This request should be made in a very positive manner, e.g. suggesting it would provide both parties an opportunity to explore areas of mutual gain.

TAKING CHARGE: Take control. Tell the employer that if you don't hear from him within a reasonable period of time you will call him to set up an interview. It is an aggressive approach. It is an aggression that shows interest. I realize in many cases it would be expensive to call every employer you send an application to. But if you can afford it, do it. (A cell phone plan with unlimited calling can be a real value here.) Whatever you do be sure to call as a reminder to those businesses you're very sure you can make a profit at. If you really are enthusiastic about getting a job, DON'T BE AFRAID TO SHOW IT. (I've always felt that I missed out on a job I would have loved because I shyly said, "Yes, I think I'd like it," when I should have jumped up and down and said, "By golly gee whiz I love doing that." Don't have any such regrets in your life.

DETAILS ABOUT POSSIBLE INTERVIEW TIMES: In some cases details about when you will be in an employer's area and available for an interview can be important. If, for example, you are only going to be in a given area for a week you will have to budget your interview time and will have to be forceful about scheduling interviews. I suggest the following guidelines.

a) Limit you interviews to two per day: one in the morning and one in the afternoon. You don't want to blow an interview by showing up late or rushing out early.

b) Offer each employer two different dates for the interview. One date should offer a morning meeting and the other an afternoon meeting.

For Example:

Bob had a two-week vacation coming up and he planned on spending them in New York interviewing for a better job. He began writing early for interviews, 3 months before his two week vacation began.

His two-week calendar included the following available dates From Monday the 31st to Friday the 11th.

Since he only had ten days his first list of potential employers consisted of ten names. These were the companies he had the most hope for.

Next to each on a sheet of paper he put the date had suggested for the morning and afternoon interview. Just in case someone might be out for the week he suggest two dates on separate weeks.

On his master sheet he used a simple code to indicate results. The brackets around the date meant an accepted interview date. An 'X' by the company name indicated that the dates were not acceptable and a '#' meant that the company was not interested in talking to him. He allowed two weeks for the company to reply before phoning the person he had written to. An 'O' meant no reply. Wornning Ware was crossed off his list, not so much because they refused to see him, but because he had not had a reply within his three week working deadline. To facilitate replies and avoid telephone expense, he sent out self-addressed stamped envelopes with his résumé.

INTERVIEW	NAME OF COMPANY	MORNING	AFTERNOON
	Tatington	[31]	11th
	Will Work	11th	[31]
	Steel Company	[1st]	10th
	Glubber Inc.	[10th]	1st
#	~~Dental Floss Inc.~~	2nd	9th
	Walton Company	[9th]	2nd
X	Green Tiger Cats	3rd	8th
X	Camel Hair Co.	8th	3rd
#	~~Swan Song Inc~~	4th	7th
O	~~Wornning Ware~~	7th	4th

In the next round of interview requests he sent out six résumés. He had thirteen available dates and this was as many as he could send out, still offering each at least two possible times. (Kingston was offered two afternoons because he had two available and it was a company he was most interested in, in this group.)

INTERVIEW	NAME OF COMPANY	MORNING	AFTERNOON
	Green Tiger Cats	11th	[1st]
	Camel Hair Co.	[2nd]	11th
#	~~Wishful Hair~~	3rd	10th
	Faliming Film	[8th]	2nd
	Grapple	4th	[8th]
	Kingston Foods	7th	3rd & [4th]

As each of his contacts accepted or rejected his interview proposals he used the same procedure over again and managed to have some time for call backs if there were any in his final schedule.

INTERVIEW	NAME OF COMPANY	MORNING	AFTERNOON
	Tatington	[31]	
	Will Work		[31]
	Steel Company	[1st]	
	Glubber Inc.	[10th]	
	Walton Company	[9th]	
	Green Tiger Cats		[1st]
	Camel Hair Co.	[2nd]	
	Faliming Film	[8th]	
	Grapple		[8th]
	Kingston Foods		[4th]

HIRE ME: Finally, your cover letter should point out your résumé says HIRE ME! Your entire cover letter should reflect that you have something to offer. One of the tenets of advertising is to repeat a message until it sinks in. By saying hire me, and backing it up with an aggressive positive attitude (not "Hire me or else!" but "I'll call your office if I don't hear from you in a few weeks.") you'll increase your chances of selling yourself.

We will see how all these aspects go together later.

HOT vs. COLD LETTERS

There are two types of cover letters. The cold letter is geared toward the company which has given no indication that a job is available. The hot letter is geared toward the company that has made it clear a job is available.

The cover letter kit which follows is geared toward the cold letter. The cold letter format is given because the cold letter can be sent to hot job prospects as well. The only difference being that in the hot letter the individual should answer whatever questions the employer has asked in his advertisement that are not answered in the résumé itself.

THE COVER LETTER KIT

Because I've found the best things keep working, I've broken down the cover letter into a collection of best components. By combining them you can make your own effective cover letter by combining them in your own way.

Start out by introducing yourself. A good way is to borrow a little from your heading.

Dear Sir:

I'm an aggressive, profit-orientated salesman who has more than doubled his volume in the past year.

or

Dear Sir:

I'm an innovative self-starter whose accomplishments in production design have saved my present company * $200,000 in the past year.

(* Note: "company" is used here instead of a specific name deliberately. This is because the phrase "Résumé submitted in confidence" is in the résumé, not in the cover letter. If you don't want your company contacted you should never mention its name without mentioning your résumé is being submitted in confidence. [There is always the chance your résumé will get lost or the prospective employer will like you so much he'll want to find out more about you right away. Don't forget Edsel Murphy's Law: if anything can go wrong, it will.] However, I feel that inserting that statement in the cover letter detracts from its sales pitch.)

It is always a good idea to repeat the message in the heading at the beginning of your cover letter. Not the entire message, but enough to indicate you are offering something of value. In some cases you may find it convenient to point out directly something that is not spelled out in your resumé heading.

Ex:

>WRITER/EDITOR
>Communication specialist with the technical background and the comprehensive ability to understand scientific material and the journalist skills to make that matter communicable on any level.

Dear Sir:

I believe that my combination of experience in both science and journalism could be of value to....

In the above example the heading refers only to skills. The cover letter points out experience.

The next item that needs to be mentioned is your resumé. Some of the phrases that might be used to introduce it are listed below.

As my enclosed resumé will show -

Outlined in my enclosed resumé -

I direct your attention to my enclosed resumé -

I'm enclosing my resumé to acquaint you with my abilities and experience -

Note the use of MY. Personal pronouns like I and my should be used in the cover letter. However, they are not often used in the resumé. Part of this is convention and part practical. The letter is intended to be a personal contact between you and the prospective employer. The resumé is a formal selling document and will sound more objective if personal pronouns are kept to a minimum.

The next step may be to give an indication you know something about the company you are applying to. Some statements that can help introduce this information are:

I've done some research on Name-of-Company....

My analysis indicates that Name-of-Company is in need of....

I've done extensive research in the field of....

THEN COMES MENTIONING THE INTERVIEW:

I would like to set up an interview at your convenience...

I'd like the opportunity to meet and discuss with you, at your convenience....

Try not to be too original. The major idea is to get the message across.

The ways to say "hire me!" are endless:

Your product line is one I feel I could sell successfully.

I feel that in a company such as yours I could use my talents most profitably.

The talent I can place at your disposal....

You may have a position for someone of my talents....

I believe I could be a highly profitable group member....

I believe my diverse expertise could be of value....

I believe my experience and ability are commensurate...

I feel that it would be a position in which I

could grow in my profession while enhancing the profits of....

I have skills, which would be of value.

I have knowledge and experience that is becoming increasingly more valuable to companies such as yours.

I do believe my record is indicative of the type of performance you can expect from me.

I believe an alliance could be mutually profitable.

Then, of course, there are the details that may have to be arranged:

I will be in your area (the name of city area) from (dates).

I would like to set up an appointment either on the morning of (date) or on the afternoon of (date). Please let me know if this is convenient to you.

The follow-up:

I will phone your office (say when) unless I hear form you by (say when).

Signature:

Yours, Yours truly, Sincerely, etc. should be used.

Then leave room between this complimentary close and your typed name for a your full signature.

Dear Robert Townsendly:

I believe that my combination of experience in both science and journalism could be of value to the Symoblical Chemical Company in your Marketing and Promotions Department.

I know from recent newspaper articles and some personal research that you are planning an expansion into new market areas.

As my enclosed résumé will show, I've had extensive experience in advertising as well as chemical research. I believe we can use my combination of expertise in a mutually profitable position within your company.

I will be in your area from August 15th to August 31st.

I would like to set up an appointment either on the morning of August 15th or on the afternoon of August 17th. Please let me know if this is convenient to you.

I will phone your office by August 10th, unless I hear form you before that.

Sincerely,

John J. Gone

TO SUM UP THE PARTS OF YOUR LETTER:

- Do some research and always write to an actual person not just personnel department.[xvii]
- Introduce yourself as someone with something to offer of value to the employer.
- Mention your knowledge of the company.
- Refer to your enclosed resume.
- Mention when you will be available for an interview and suggest dates.
- Say you will contact the employer if you don't hear from the employer.
- Sign it.

THE RÉSUMÉ COVER LETTER COMBINATION

The effective combination of your résumé and cover letter depend on the working relationship between the general advertisement and your personal contact. Your cover letter should tell an individual that you feel their job is one you had in mind when you wrote the résumé. If this is done correctly one résumé can be used for different types of jobs, i.e. with a generalized objective at the top (Management, Sales, etc.) and a cover letter that says this is exactly the kind of job I was referring to.

SOME CONCLUDING NOTES

BLIND-BOX ADS

Beware of blind-box ads if you're employed and don't want your employer to know you've been looking. Not only might the ad belong to your employer but also the anonymous ad placer has less need not to be careless in contacting your present employer.

Some blind-box ads don't even have jobs behind them. Some people place ads asking for some type of help just to find out who is available and how much they are asking.

I've even told a few clients they might try placing their own blind-box ad to find out who is competing against them in their job market. They place a blind-box ad asking for applicants to the same sort of job they are looking for. What they get is an idea of the competition in the field along with an idea of what these people want in terms of salary. This can give you a very competitive edge. Such blind box-ads, however, should be worded carefully. False advertising can be a misdemeanor in some areas. But then you don't actually have to say there is a job.[xviii]

SOURCES OF COMPANIES:

In addition to the internet, I usually suggest the phone book in local areas of the local city directory. City directories are nice as they usually list the important people in the company. Another source is Standard and Poor's DIRECTORY OF AMERICAN CORPORATIONS. This book lists corporations by state. Unfortunately the company may not be listed in your state if the main office is elsewhere. However, it is an excellent reference as it describers the company and lists its officers.

But the best source of information is the reference librarian at your local library. These people are paid to find information for you. And most are very happy to help job hunters.

TECHNICAL

Type your résumé or have it typed and use a quality ink-jet or laser printer, or have it printed by an offset printing press[xix] or high-quality copy shop. NOTHING ELSE WILL DO. You'll be competing for a job so it pays to look your best.

Print your résumé on the best paper you can find. Although 20 lb. bond is okay, a nicer heavier paper may add to the appearance of your résumé and be slightly more impressive. If you decide to have your résumé printed professionally shop around for printers. Quick print places can be found almost anywhere, but do some comparison shopping. Due to advances in technology copy shops can often match the quality of offset printing so include them in the comparison.

When mailing your résumé simply fold it with the cover letter and stick it in an envelope. But if presenting it in person you might be better off using an inexpensive folder of some sort. There are imitation leather ones, plastic ones, etc. and they do make a good impression when you are handing a résumé to someone. The only reason I don't suggest you send them thru the mail is they are expensive to mail.

LETTERS OF RECOMMENDATION

If you do have letters from your past employer sometimes it can help to send them along with the résumé. This does of course break the rule of no references but if the letter is a glowing one the prospective employer will probably only check to see if it is real.

COMPANY LETTERHEADS

If you are leaving because your job is being terminated but your company is happy with you they might let you use their letterhead. Do so. But try a few without the letterhead and compare response.

SUMMING UP
I've never had a résumé customer who was not successful. If you have the proper job finding attitude: Hire me because then we will both profit, and put your qualifications in a well developed résumé cover letter combination, you will, if you keep trying, find a job.

FINALLY
Don't forget to thank your references when you get a job. You may need them again someday. And thank you for reading this -book.

                                                 The End

APPENDIX

The following is a sample of the questions I had on the form I used to collect information about my clients. I've included it here because filling it out might help you get started in collecting information about yourself.

Full Name
Address
Telephone
Marital Status
Dependents
Age
Height
Weight
General Health
High School
    dates attended
    Graduated?
College
    dates attended
    Major-Minor Degree?
Grad School
    Dates Attended
    Major
    Degree?
Title of Dissertation
Scholarships
    % of College $ earned
Evening Classes
Trade, Correspondence Schools
Company Sponsored Classes or Seminars Attended
Honor Societies
Fraternities
Dates of Military Duty
    Draft Status
    Location of Duty
    Military School
    Military Duties
    Rank in - Rank out
Professional Affiliation (society, grade, years, offices held)
Patents & Publications
Professional Awards
Languages   (include computer languages)

```
            Speak
            Read
            Write
      Employment Record (List employers in reverse
      chronological order)
      Current Employer:
      Address:
      Position Held:
      Supervisor:
      May Employer or supervisor be contacted?
      Dates of Employment:
      Salary, beginning:
            Ending:
      Describe Chief Duties:
      Reason for required change:
      Past Employer:
      Address:
      Position Held:
      Supervisor:
      May Employer or supervisor be contacted?
      Dates of Employment:
      Salary, beginning:
            Ending:
      Describe Chief Duties:
      Reason for required change:


      The end
```

---

[i] Not all jobs are advertised. It is not a bad idea to send write companies who may need your special abilities, but have not advertised a position.

[ii] I dropped out of Grad school in Chemistry here. I have two masters' degrees, an MFA in creative writing and an MA in Interpersonal Communication. I have undergraduate degrees in journalism and chemistry.

[iii] Unless you are a journalism major applying for a job, you may use numbers or letters. If you are a journalist use the style book the paper you are applying to uses.

[iv] See the boy's club coach example shown earlier.

[v] Most experts feel that networking (or if you don't have a network, cold calls) are the best source of jobs.

[vi] Do not submit a 4 page résumé if the job description asks for 1 page, even if you are applying to be company president.

[vii] Never allow yourself to be limited by ads for jobs. You should be constantly contacting companies that have the kind of position you desire whether they are advertising such a position or not.

[viii] Groups have a tendency to hold individuals to the group's norm.

[ix] I personally filed a complaint with the State Department of Labor against a company that discriminated, I felt, because of age. It was a waste of time. Though the company did, however, change its policy in the future.

[x] Way back when I was in grad school as a chemist I applied for a research chemist's position. I was young and had no idea what to ask for as a salary. I named a figure and never heard back. I heard later they hired someone for 75% of what I was asking. Later, when I did have a job, I recommended a guy I knew for a new position. The personnel manger called me to my office and angrily demanded to know if I had told this guy to ask for 133% of what I was making. Try to find out what the going salaries are for people with your level of experience in your field.

[xi] My first job was as a chemist for Revlon. At the time people were, in fact, booted out the day they gave notice to prevent them from collecting company secrets to take to their new job.

[xii] High risk hobbies like sky diving might be better saved to mention at another time. If an employer things sky diving is very dangerous they may think: Why hire someone who might not last long?

[xiii] Your office supply store can help you chose paper for your printer. Not all combinations are compatible. For example, laser gloss paper can look impressive but will not work with an ink-jet printer.

[xiv] Putting written work aside to get some distance from it before proofreading is a good way to avoid errors. If you proofread too soon, you are more likely to imagine things are okay which are not.

[xv] For some reason more and more online phone number searches seem to lead to companies that want to charge you for the information. It is possible, as if this writing, with diligence to find a free listing, but the companies that charge seem to take up pages and pages of listing that are so-called 'free' but are not. Then again, even phone directory assistance is not free. You may save yourself time and energy by buying a monthly plan, even if only for one month, that helps you quickly find all the phone numbers you'll need.

[xvi] Do use job service. For example, I came across a government grant that funds a training program for people 55 and older. That is the government will pay the over 55 year old applicant's salary (or a portion) while that person is learning the job. To be in this program you have to go through a local job service.

[xvii] You can always call the company and ask for a name.

[xviii] I confess that years ago I did some writing for "The National Enquirer." One of the stories they wanted from me was "Where people hide their valuables according to a burglar." I gave them the idea, and only when they accepted, did I realize I didn't know how to find a burglar. So I used a blind box ad and was very glad I had. One guy, I did not interview, sent me his rap sheet. He had been arrested for rape, attempted murder, assault and battery, etc. He said it was hard for him to get this rap sheet so I'd better get it back to him. There was no way I was going to contact someone like that. (For you job hunters it is probably best not to send your rap sheet.)

[xix] Small offset printing shops are vanishing due to high quality printer and copy shops with high-tech equipment.